First History Encyclopedia

Project editor Manisha Majithia
Senior art editor Ann Cannings
Editor Kathleen Teece
Editorial assistants Shalini Agrawal, Katie Lawrence,
Abigail Luscombe, Mark Silas
Design Radhika Banerjee, Jim Green,
Emma Hobson, Xiao Lin, Roohi Rais, Lucy Sims
DTP designers Sachin Gupta, Vikram Singh
Picture researcher Aditya Katyal
Jacket co-ordinator Issy Walsh
Jacket designer Dheeraj Arora
Managing editors Laura Gilbert,
Alka Thakur Hazarika
Deputy managing art editor Ivy Sengupta
Managing art editor Diane Peyton Jones
Producer Inderjit Bhullar
Senior pre-producer Nikoleta Parasaki
Delhi team head Malavika Talukder
Creative director Helen Senior
Publishing director Sarah Larter

Author Philip Wilkinson
Consultant Peter Chrisp

First published in Great Britain in 2019
by Dorling Kindersley Limited
80 Strand, London, WC2R 0RL

Copyright © 2019 Dorling Kindersley Limited
A Penguin Random House Company
10 9 8 7 6 5 4 3 2 1
001–313250–Aug/2019

All rights reserved.
No part of this publication may be reproduced, stored
in or introduced into a retrieval system, or transmitted,
in any form, or by any means (electronic, mechanical,
photocopying, recording, or otherwise), without the
prior written permission of the copyright owner.

A CIP catalogue record for this book
is available from the British Library.
ISBN 978-0-2414-3490-1

Printed and bound in India

A WORLD OF IDEAS:
SEE ALL THERE IS TO KNOW

www.dk.com

Contents

Introduction

The Ancient World

The Classical World

The Medieval World

There is a question at the bottom of each page...

Every page is colour-coded to show you which section it is in.

Did you know? These buttons give extra fascinating facts about history.

About this book
The pages of this book have special features that will show you how to get your hands on as much information as possible!

BCE/CE
When you see the letters BCE, it means Before the Common Era, which began in the year 1 CE (Common Era).

What is history?

History is the study of the past. There are different types of history, such as military history, about wars, and social history, about the way people lived. We can learn about the past from evidence, such as objects, writings, and other sources of information.

Film and photographs

Old photographs and films can be used as historical evidence. They show us what people wore, where they lived, and what they did in their spare time.

Archaeology

Archaeology is the study of history by looking at, or by digging up, historical sites to find remains left behind by people in the past. People who dig up and study these remains are called archaeologists.

This decorated ancient Greek amphora (wine jar) dates back to around 600–500 BCE.

Museums

Museums are places that store objects used by people from the past. Curators are the people who choose the items to display in museums. They research these objects and write about them, to help visitors to the museum understand how they were used.

4

Buildings

Old houses and their designs are quite different from houses built today. They give us a good idea of what life was like before modern technology, when everything had to be made by hand.

18th-century houses, like this manor house in Estonia, are very different from modern houses.

Madonna and Child, painting by Carlo Crivelli (1480)

Documents

Historians (people who study history) use written documents, such as ancient books and diaries, to find out about life in earlier times. Writing is so important to the study of history that the period before it was invented is called prehistory (before history).

Art

Art, such as paintings, drawings, and sculptures can show us lots of things about history. A painting might show us what the houses, landscape, or clothing of the time looked like.

Handwritten postcards about sea travel written in the early 20th century

People

Memories are some of the best sources for the history of more recent events. Oral (spoken word) historians study history by talking to people and writing down what they say.

Anyone can study history. You are doing so, by reading this book.

Early humans

The first humans came from apes who lived around 6 million years ago. Our earliest human relatives are called hominins. Over time, many types, or species, of hominin appeared, gradually becoming more like the humans we are today.

The first hominins

Our earliest human relatives were apes who began to walk on two legs, and got smarter as their brains grew larger. Modern humans like us appeared around 200,000 years ago.

Australopithecus was a short, small-brained species of hominin that lived in Africa between 4 and 2 million years ago.

Tool-makers

Around 3 million years ago, hominins learned to make tools out of stone. The earliest stone tools that have been found were made in Africa, and were used for chopping or cutting.

Hand-axes were invented around 1.7 million years ago.

Small, sharp stone points snapped off from stone blades

People hunted mammoths for their meat and warm skins.

6

How do we know what animals lived during the Ice Age?

Hearths

A round stick called a drill was rubbed against a flat piece of wood called a hearth to produce a spark.

Drill

Fire

Early humans learned how to make fire by rubbing pieces of wood together quickly. Fire-making was a useful skill, as fires could be used to cook meat, help keep people warm, and scare away dangerous animals.

Fires were kept alight with sticks and held together by round stones.

Ice Age

During an Ice Age, temperatures become so cold that ice covers large parts of the Earth. The last Ice Age began around 110,000 years ago, lasting until 10,000 BCE. People had to make warmer shelters and find new foods, as some plants no longer grew because of the cold weather.

The woolly mammoth was an animal that lived during the Ice Age.

Layers of deer skins overlap to make the shelter warm and waterproof.

Shelter made of wooden poles and deer skins

Shelter

When the weather got too cold, people needed to live in warm shelters, or homes. They lived in caves, or made houses out of wood or the warm, waterproof skins of animals, such as mammoths or deer.

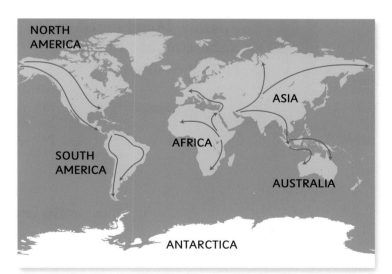

NORTH AMERICA

ASIA

AFRICA

SOUTH AMERICA

AUSTRALIA

ANTARCTICA

Map showing early hominins' journeys out of Africa

Leaving Africa

Our early human relatives lived in Africa. From here, they travelled long distances to Asia, Europe, Australia, and America. In some places, different species of early human lived side by side.

We have found animal remains frozen in ice and drawings of animals on cave walls.

Stone Age

The Stone Age was the period when our earliest human relatives began to make stone tools for the first time. They also developed key skills such as farming and building, which we still use today. The Stone Age started around 3.3 million years ago and ended around 4,000 years ago.

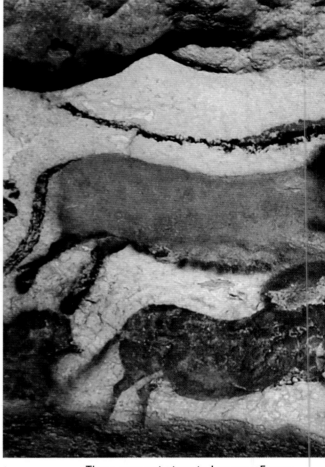

These cave paintings in Lascaux, France, are more than 15,000 years old.

Hunting and gathering

People travelled long distances to find food. Stone Age women and children gathered and cooked plants. Men hunted animals and caught fish with stone weapons.

This type of spear with a sharp stone tip was used to kill animals for food.

Arrowheads made of stone

Clothing made of animal skins

Farming

By around 9000 BCE, people started to plant crops, such as peas and lentils. They also raised animals, such as sheep and goats, which provided a supply of milk and wool.

Goat's wool would have kept Stone Age people warm in cold weather.

Did Stone Age people live in caves?

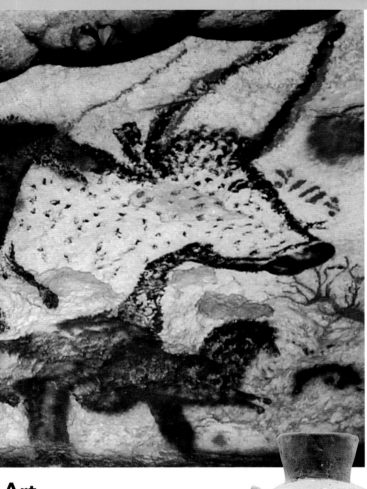

Spinning and weaving

By pulling and twisting material, such as wool, people made thread for sewing. Later, they learned how to weave these threads together to make pieces of cloth.

Bone needle and thread used for sewing

Spinning whorl

A spindle stick was placed inside the whorl. Wool was attached to the stick. Spinning the whorl twisted the wool into thread.

Houses

Some Stone Age people made houses out of wood and mud. In other places, where there were few trees, people built houses with stones. The weight and shape of the stones held the houses together.

Art

Stone Age people made lots of art. They decorated objects with patterns and drawings, or painted animals and human figures on rocks and cave walls. They made colours from mud or burned wood.

Painted Stone Age pot

This house, from the Stone Age village of Skara Brae in the modern-day Orkney Islands off the coast of Scotland, was built around 3000 BCE.

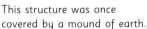

This structure was once covered by a mound of earth.

Poulnabrone, an ancient megalithic tomb in Ireland

Beliefs

Stone Age people built stone structures called megaliths. Many megaliths were built as tombs for the dead. Stone circles and temples were also built during the Stone Age. Religious ceremonies were held here.

9

Some did, but most lived in places where there were no caves.

Mesopotamia

Mesopotamia means "the land between two rivers". It was here, from 4500 BCE, that the world's first cities were built between the rivers Tigris and Euphrates (in modern-day Iraq). Each city was ruled by a king.

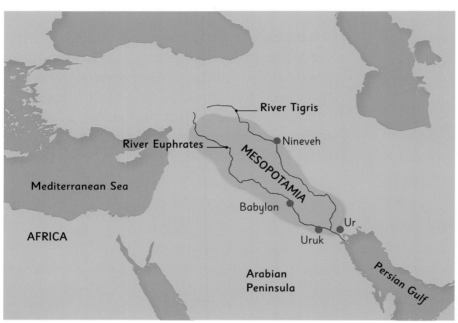

Writing

This clay slab is covered in cuneiform writing.

The Mesopotamians invented one of the earliest types of writing called cuneiform, which means wedge-shaped. They wrote by pressing reeds (strong, tall grass) into soft clay.

Religion

Cities, such as Ur and Uruk, had their own special gods. They were worshipped in huge temples made out of brick, called ziggurats. These temples were run by priests, who could read and write.

Fertile lands

People lived by the rivers as the land was made fertile (good for growing crops) by river water. This helped them grow lots of food, such as barley. Many of the main Mesopotamian cities, such as Babylon, were built by a river.

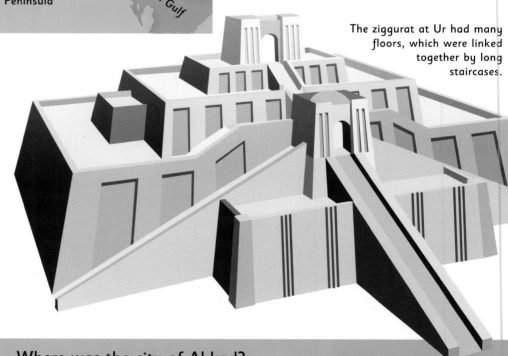

The ziggurat at Ur had many floors, which were linked together by long staircases.

Where was the city of Akkad?

Babylon

In around 1750 BCE, Babylon became the most powerful city in Mesopotamia. The Babylonian king Hammurabi was a powerful leader who made strict laws. These were carved into stone pillars so people could always see them.

The Ishtar Gate was one of eight main entrances into Babylon. It was covered in colourful bricks and used as a starting point for religious processions.

Heroic Tales

The earliest surviving long poem is *The Epic of Gilgamesh*. It is a poem that tells the story of a Mesopotamian king called Gilgamesh. His adventures include fights with monsters and a journey to the Underworld.

Bronze head of an Akkadian ruler, thought to be Sargon

Akkadian Empire

The city of Akkad became powerful under a king called Sargon in around 2330 BCE. Legends say he was a poor man who rose to be king of Akkad, and then conquered most of Mesopotamia.

This statue may show Gilgamesh wrestling a lion.

11

Indus Valley civilization

Some of the world's first cities were built around 5,000 years ago in what is now Pakistan and India. This was the Indus Valley civilization. These peaceful city-dwellers wove cotton, traded (or swapped) goods with distant lands, and created one of the first writing systems.

Trade

Items such as cotton cloth and beads were often traded for goods from elsewhere, such as the precious metal gold. Goods were traded with people from areas such as Mesopotamia, which was in the Middle East.

Different seals placed with traded goods may have let people know who the trader was.

Clay seal

Stone blocks used to check the weight of goods

Cities

Straight streets ran alongside each other in cities such as Mohenjo-Daro and Harappa. Buildings had multiple floors, and human waste flowed from homes into underground drains.

Mohenjo-Daro was one of the largest Indus Valley cities.

Rubbish was dumped in an area outside the city to keep the streets clean.

The mud-bricks were carefully laid to make thick, strong walls that kept out the heat.

What does the Indus Valley writing tell us about the cities?

Necklace of
agate beads

Arts and crafts
Indus Valley craft workers
produced beautiful metalwork,
polished beads made from stones
such as agate and turquoise, and
clay figures that may have been
used as toys or ornaments.

Headband with
circular ornament

Terracotta (baked clay)
figure of an animal

Gold
jewellery

Religion
The civilization's religion
remains a mystery. It could
have included one god or
many. A figure thought to
be a priest-king has been
found, but we don't know
who he really was.

Patterned cloak
(once painted red)

Priest-king sculpture

The building on this mound
overlooked the city. It may
have housed a government
or been the site of public
meetings and gatherings.

Where did they go?
By about 1700 BCE, people had left the cities
empty. The Indus River may have changed
course, stopping a twice-yearly flood that
watered fields and helped crops grow.

Very little, as modern scholars cannot read it!

Papyrus was a plant that grew by the river. The Egyptians made baskets, boats, and a paper-like writing material from papyrus.

Ancient Egypt

The civilization of ancient Egypt began in around 3000 BCE and lasted almost 3,000 years. The River Nile runs through Egypt, with desert on each side. Almost all ancient Egyptians lived by the river to be close to water, as there was none in the desert.

Turn and learn
Fertile lands
pp. 10–11

River Nile

The River Nile stretches from the top to the bottom of Egypt and then further south into Sudan. It gave Egyptians a transport route, a source of fish, and a supply of drinking water.

River Nile

Boats could be made from wood or papyrus.

Did Egyptian women wear make-up?

Egyptian farmer using a plough (farming tool) pulled by oxen

Farming

Every year the Nile flooded, carrying mud and fine sand, called silt, onto the fields nearby. Silt made the land fertile, or good for growing crops. Egyptian farmers were able to grow wheat, barley, vegetables, figs, and grapes.

Grapes

Bread

Figs

The people on this Nile boat are hunting birds and catching fish. Other boats carried goods and livestock.

Food

People ate a lot of flatbread, which they made with wheat or barley. They had figs or melon as dessert, and they crushed grapes to make wine.

Clothing

Ancient Egyptian clothes were made of linen, a cloth that comes from fibres of the flax plant. People liked linen because it kept them cool in the hot Egyptian weather.

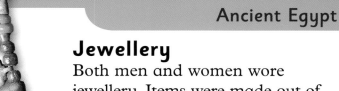

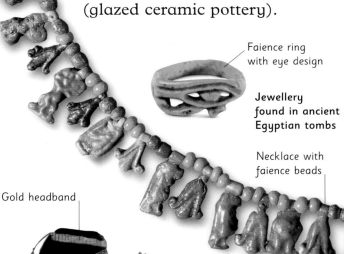

Jewellery

Both men and women wore jewellery. Items were made out of gold, as well as cheaper materials such as stones, glass, and faience (glazed ceramic pottery).

Faience ring with eye design

Jewellery found in ancient Egyptian tombs

Necklace with faience beads

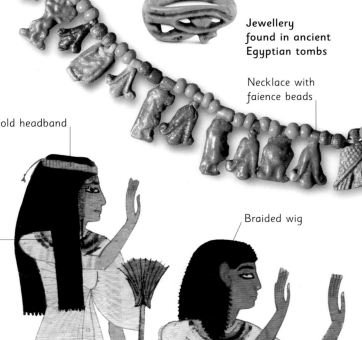

Gold headband

Beaded necklace

Braided wig

This fabric has many folds. It moves easily as the person walks.

Dress made of very thin linen

Wooden oar for steering

Women had long dresses and men wore tunics.

Yes, and many men did too.

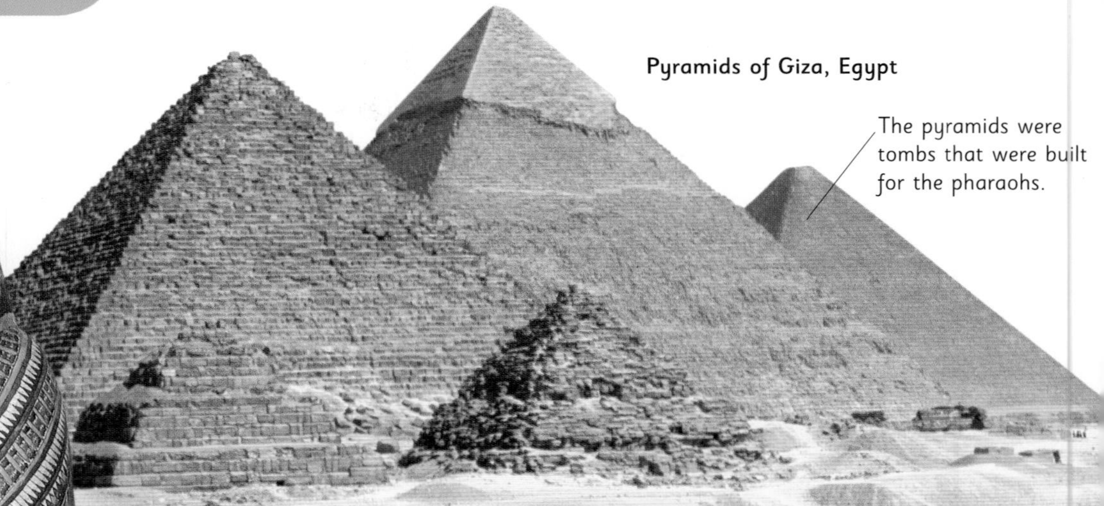

Pyramids of Giza, Egypt

The pyramids were tombs that were built for the pharaohs.

Egyptian kings

Ancient Egyptian kings were called pharaohs. People believed they were as powerful as gods. When a pharaoh died, his body was kept in a good condition as people believed that he would need it to join the other gods in the afterlife.

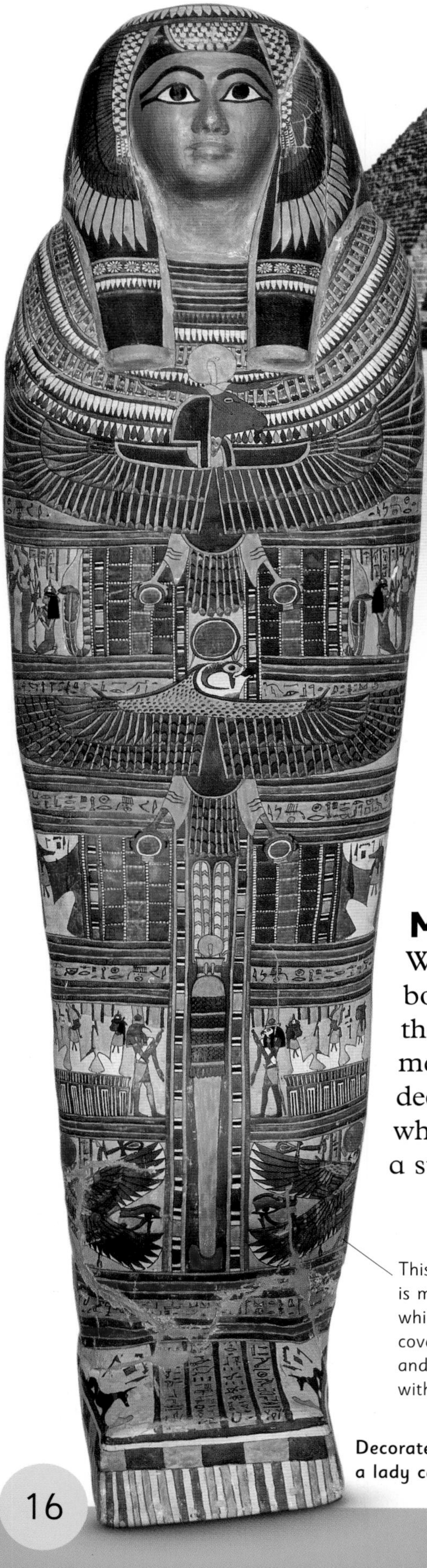

This temple was cut into the rock of a cliff face.

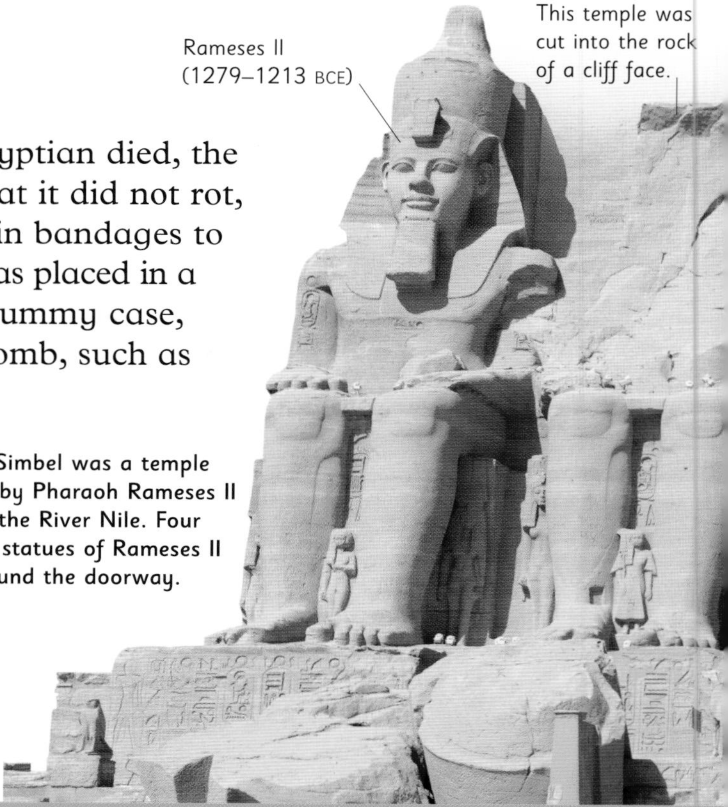

Rameses II (1279–1213 BCE)

Mummies

When an ancient Egyptian died, the body was dried so that it did not rot, then it was wrapped in bandages to make a mummy. It was placed in a decorated coffin, or mummy case, which was kept in a tomb, such as a stone pyramid.

This mummy case is made of linen, which has been covered with plaster and decorated with paint.

Abu Simbel was a temple built by Pharaoh Rameses II near the River Nile. Four huge statues of Rameses II surround the doorway.

Decorated mummy case of a lady called Takhenmes

16

Painted stone showing the Sun god Re-Harakhty (left)

Gods and goddesses

The Egyptians worshipped hundreds of gods and goddesses. The chief god was the Sun god, who took several different forms. Often, he was a hawk-like creature called Re-Harakhty. Ancient Egyptians believed they could join the gods in the afterlife once they had died.

A person brings offerings to Re-Harakhty.

Hieroglyphs

Scribes were educated people who worked for the pharaoh or the temples. They wrote in symbols called hieroglyphs, which were little pictures that stood for words, sounds, or ideas.

Egyptian hieroglyphs carved into stone

Pharaohs of Egypt

The pharaohs ruled the whole of Egypt. They showed their power by having huge temples built to the gods. These often had enormous statues of the pharaoh on the outside.

Tutankhamun (1332–1322 BCE) became a pharaoh when he was just a boy. We know a lot about him because his tomb was discovered full of his belongings. His mummy had a beautiful mask that was made of blue glass and gold.

Mostly for religious writing. Scribes used an easier script called hieratic for other writing.

Bronze Age

The Bronze Age began about 5,500 years ago when people first learned how to make bronze by mixing two metals, copper and tin. They used bronze to make weapons and tools. The use of bronze quickly spread throughout Europe and other parts of the world.

Western Europe
(2000 BCE)

The Aegean
(3000 BCE)

Mesopotamia,
western Asia
(3300 BCE)

Egypt
(3200 BCE)

Early Bronze Age civilizations

Where in the world?

Bronze working started in different places at different times. People first learned to make bronze in western Asia. Its use spread first to Egypt and then to Europe.

Settlements

In Bronze Age Europe, people lived together in large villages called settlements. Their homes were built with local materials, such as wood.

The houses are built on stilts above the water of a lake and have wooden frames.

Reconstructed Bronze Age houses in Germany

Roof of wooden tiles

Why did people add tin to copper when making bronze?

Bronze Age in China

From the 16th to 11th centuries BCE, bronze making became widespread in China, where people made objects such as bowls and cups. This period is known as the Shang Dynasty.

Bronze *gu* (drinking cup) made during the Shang Dynasty

How was bronze made?

Ores, or rocks containing copper and tin, were heated to turn the metals inside to liquid. These were mixed together to make bronze, then poured into a mould to cool and set into shape.

Mould for making bronze pins

Tin ore

Copper ore

Bronze pin made in mould

Brooch found in the Carpathian basin in Central Europe

Bronze pendant

Jewellery

Bronze jewellery was popular in Europe. Bronze Age people traded goods for finely patterned bronze bracelets and brooches. Bronze jewellery was originally a shiny yellow colour, but over thousands of years has faded to a dull green.

Spearhead

Bronze helmet from Central Europe

Weapons

People made axe-heads, spearheads, and other weapons from bronze. They could be sharpened and repaired when they were damaged, unlike stone weapons.

Axe-head

Helmet made of two pieces of bronze

Image of a wheeled chariot set into the side of a wooden box found in Ur, Mesopotamia

The wheel

People invented the wheel during the Bronze Age. Wheels were used to build chariots and carts that could move around easily when horses pulled them.

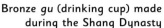

Ancient China

From around 475 BCE, China was divided into several kingdoms that were always at war with one another. These kingdoms were united to form the huge empire of China in 221 BCE, when Shi Huangdi, the first emperor, defeated all of his rivals and took control of ancient China.

Emperors

The first emperor, Shi Huangdi, came from Qin, a kingdom in western China. He conquered the whole of China with his huge army, and then built a great wall to keep enemies out and a long canal to improve transport through the country.

Portrait of Shi Huangdi

Coins

People of ancient China had to use bronze coins that were approved by the emperor. These coins had the same value across China, and they were all round with a square hole in the centre.

Chinese coins from around 210 BCE

Beliefs

The Chinese believed that their gods were able to predict the future. They wrote questions for the gods on animal bones or turtle shells, then heated them. The heat cracked the bones and priests interpreted, or read, messages in the cracks.

Questions written in Chinese on the turtle shell

12 characters written in the Qin style

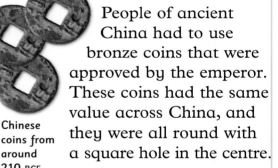

A turtle shell that priests used to tell the future

Writing

Shi Huangdi made everyone use the type of writing used in Qin, so people from one side of China to the other could understand each other easily.

Stone slab with Qin writing

Were any animals buried with the Terracotta Army?

The Great Wall

Shi Huangdi ordered his soldiers to build a wall made out of earth along China's northern borders to protect the country from enemies. During the Ming dynasty in the 15th century CE, the wall was rebuilt with stone to make it stronger. This wall is the Great Wall of China.

The Great Wall of China is 8,850 km (5,500 miles) long.

The terracotta soldiers are life-sized statues.

Terracotta Army

When Shi Huangdi died, he was buried in a large underground tomb, along with around 7,000 statues of his soldiers to protect him in the afterlife. The soldiers were made from terracotta, a type of pottery.

Yes, 670 terracotta horses were buried in Shi Huangdi's tomb.

Ancient Greece

Ancient Greek civilization was at its height between 500 and 300 BCE. The ancient Greeks had a huge effect on people who came after them. They wrote books that are still read today and influenced our art, maths, and buildings. They even invented democracy (rule by the people).

Athens

Most Greeks lived in city-states, each with its own leaders and laws. The richest and most powerful in the 5th century BCE was Athens. It was the first place in the world to have a form of democracy, and was a city where the arts and learning thrived.

Architecture

The Greeks created a style of architecture that is still used today. It was based on three different kinds of column.

Doric columns had a very plain square stone at the top.

Ionic columns were topped with a spiral design.

Corinthian columns were the most decorative, with carved leaves at the top.

The *agora*, a big market place in the middle of Athens, was a place where people shopped and met their friends.

Turn and learn
The Renaissance
pp. 76–77

How old were Spartan boys when they were sent to training camp?

Barley

Olives

Grapes

Food
The Greeks grew olives, grapes, and grain for bread. They made wine from the grapes, which both adults and children drank.

Most clothes were made of linen.

Clothes
Greek clothes were very simple. They were made of plain, rectangular pieces of cloth. The garments hung loose, so people could stay cool in the hot sunshine. Men's clothes were usually shorter than women's.

Coloured fabric was more expensive, so it was usually worn by the rich.

Sparta
Sparta was a city in southern Greece and was Athens' greatest rival. It had a strong army, because every Spartan boy had to leave their family home to train to be a soldier with other boys. Sparta won a war with Athens in the late 5th century BCE.

Greek black-figure plate showing warriors in battle

Ships and boats
Many Greeks lived near the sea. They used sailing boats for fishing and travel, and had big ships for warfare. These warships had both sails and oars, so they could travel fast, even when there was no wind.

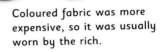

A trireme had three rows of oars on each side.

At the front was a ram, to damage enemy ships.

23

Most boys were sent to train as soldiers from the age of seven.

Greek religion and culture

Zeus is often shown carrying a king's sceptre (royal staff).

Zeus, king of the gods, and god of the sky and thunder

Cities in ancient Greece had lots of different buildings, from marble temples to theatres. The ancient Greeks built sports stadiums that held thousands of people. Many of the buildings were decorated with beautiful works of art, for which Greece was famous.

Coin showing the head of Athena, goddess of war and wisdom

Gods and goddesses

The Greeks believed that their gods and goddesses, although very powerful, were like humans. They looked like men and women, and behaved in a similar way. They had arguments and fell in and out of love.

Temples

Behind the rows of columns of a Greek temple was a large room containing a statue of a god or goddess. People brought presents for the god in the form of food or wine.

The temple of the goddess Athena in Athens

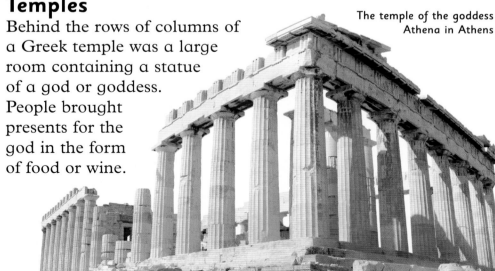

An eagle was said to carry messages for Zeus.

Did the athletes win medals at the Olympic Games?

Theatre

Plays were performed in the open air, in big round-shaped theatres. They were designed so that people sitting at the back could hear every word. The Greeks staged the first comedies (funny plays) and tragedies (plays with sad endings).

Greek actors wore different masks according to which part they were playing.

The theatre at the ancient city of Epidaurus

Pottery portraying a battle scene between the Greeks and the Amazons

Lyres usually had seven strings, played by plucking.

Entertainment

The Greeks loved music, dancing, and going to banquets, where there was lots of food to eat. They invented a popular musical instrument called the lyre, which is like a harp.

This bowl was used for mixing wine and water together, to make the wine weaker so that it lasted longer.

This lyre has a tortoise shell to make the strings sound louder.

Lyre

Pottery

The potters of ancient Greece made some of the most beautiful bowls, jars, cups, and plates ever produced. Many were decorated with fine drawings of gods, heroes, and animals.

Olympic Games

The Greek Olympics were held at a festival celebrating the god Zeus. They were held at Olympia, where his main temple stood. Athletes came from all over Greece to compete, while about 50,000 people would watch.

Statue of athlete poised to throw a discus

No, the winners were presented with a wreath of leaves.

Persian Empire

The Persians were people from modern-day Iran who created a huge and powerful empire in western Asia in the 6th century BCE. The Persian emperor was in control of the whole empire, but he had help from local rulers who looked after different parts of the empire.

Cyrus the Great
Cyrus the Great was the first Persian emperor, ruling from 549–530 BCE. He conquered lands across Asia, founding one of the biggest empires of the time.

Persepolis
The city of Persepolis was the capital city of the Persian Empire. It was a centre for rituals and ceremonies as the emperor's royal palace was here.

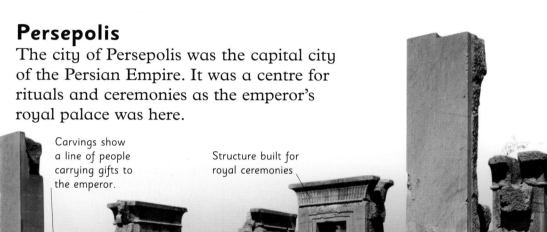

Carvings show a line of people carrying gifts to the emperor.

Structure built for royal ceremonies

When did people from different parts of the Persian Empire go to Persepolis?

Roads and transport

The Persians built one of the world's first road networks. These roads allowed people to travel easily by chariot from one part of the empire to another.

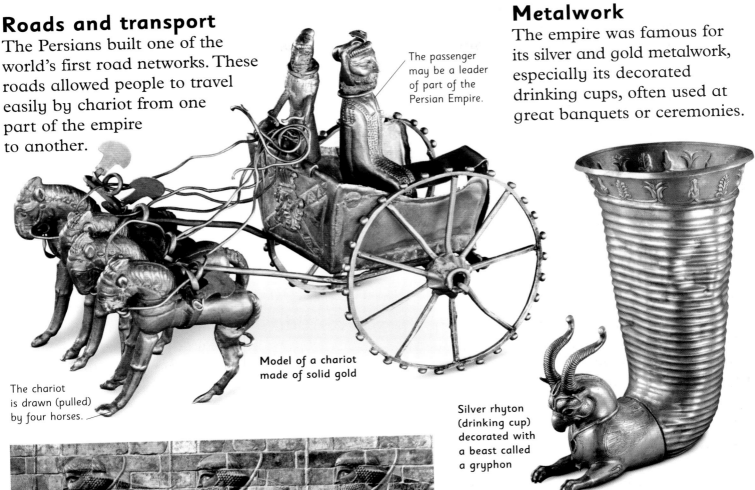

The passenger may be a leader of part of the Persian Empire.

Model of a chariot made of solid gold

The chariot is drawn (pulled) by four horses.

Metalwork

The empire was famous for its silver and gold metalwork, especially its decorated drinking cups, often used at great banquets or ceremonies.

Silver rhyton (drinking cup) decorated with a beast called a gryphon

Glazed bricks showing palace guards, from the palace in the city of Susa

Carved panel showing the symbol of Ahura Mazda

Mighty conquerors

The Persians' large well-trained army helped them to conquer many lands, and they gathered more troops in each of the places they conquered. The soldiers were also guards for the emperor's palace.

Religion

The main religion of Persia was called Zoroastrianism. It was based on the teachings of the prophet Zoroaster. Zoroastrians believed in one god, Ahura Mazda (the "Wise Lord").

Only at Persian New Year, which was celebrated at the beginning of spring.

Ancient Rome

Coin showing Julius Caesar (45–44 BCE), ruler of Rome before the emperors

By the 1st century BCE, the Romans had built one of the world's largest empires. Their talent for organization and the power of their army kept the empire together. The Roman Empire was ruled by an emperor from 27 BCE onwards.

Empire and conquests

The Romans conquered most of western Europe and large parts of western Asia and North Africa. They introduced their own culture, such as coins and style of clothing, to most of these places.

This flag shows the name of the legion (army group) these troops belonged to.

This group are using the *testudo* (Latin for "tortoise") formation, to move forwards safely in a "shell" during battle.

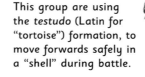

Statue of Augustus (27 BCE–14 CE), the first Roman emperor

Emperors

Roman emperors used their power in different ways. Trajan conquered new lands while Hadrian, who came after him, spent more time defending the empire's borders.

Army

The Roman army was huge, well organized, and well trained. The men were generously paid. They fought battles, but also guarded the empire's borders and worked on big projects, such as building roads.

When did the Roman Empire reach its biggest size?

Gladiators

The emperors kept people entertained with shows featuring fights between gladiators. Gladiators were usually slaves or criminals who were trained to fight to the death. They were sometimes freed if they survived.

Gladiators fought in large arenas, such as the Colosseum in Rome.

Shields overlap to protect men from enemies' weapons.

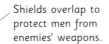

Did you know?

Some free men who liked to fight chose to become gladiators.

A round shield protects the gladiator's upper body.

Padding covers the gladiator's legs.

Master builders

The Romans built temples, aqueducts (bridges or tunnels that carry water), and other structures all over their empire. These buildings were strong and well made.

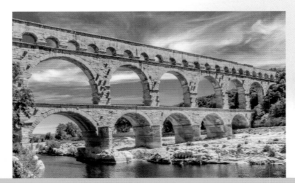

The Pont du Gard, an aqueduct that brought water to the city of Nîmes, France

29

Large Roman bath in the city of Bath, UK

Roman baths

Most Romans had no running water in their homes, so they went to public baths to wash. They began with a hot bath, or went into a dry, hot room like a sauna, and then had a cold bath to cool down. The baths were a place to meet up with friends as well as get clean.

Roman life

The Roman way of life spread all over Europe and beyond. The Romans shared their customs, food, social classes, and buildings with the whole empire. The rich usually ate many types of expensive meat and fish, but the poor had to eat plain foods, such as bread.

Citizen women had rights but were not allowed to vote in elections.

Slaves worked on farms or in citizens' homes.

Women often wore a long dress called a stola.

Slaves usually wore plain and cheaply made clothes such as this short tunic.

Citizens and slaves

There were different groups of people who lived in the Roman Empire. These groups had different rights. Slaves had no freedom and were owned by other people. Citizens had lots of rights, good jobs, and money.

What was the most popular Roman entertainment?

Writing

The language used by the Romans is called Latin. It is no longer spoken, but it is written with the same capital letters we still use today. These letters were good for carved signs, as they were easy to read.

Fast food

The Romans ate foods they could hunt and grow, such as fish and olives. They also invented "fast food", as they had street bars that served fried fish and meat, similar to the fast food restaurants we have today.

Olives from Italy

Fish from the Mediterranean Sea

Snail from France

Citizen men could vote, own property, and work in the government.

This man is wearing a toga, which is a long woollen garment.

Ruins of a two-storey block of flats in Ostia, near Rome

Brick walls

Roman homes

Some Romans had large houses built in the countryside, but many lived in flats in crowded cities. Blocks of flats usually had lots of storeys (floors). The rooms were small and flats had no kitchens or bathrooms.

Mosaics (pictures made of tiny pieces of tile) decorated the floors in some houses.

Pompeii

The town of Pompeii in southern Italy was buried by ash when Mount Vesuvius, a volcano, erupted in 79 CE. Pompeii was preserved in ash, which means we can see some of what was there before the eruption.

Iron Age

During the Iron Age, people began using iron to make tools and weapons as it was very strong and easy to find. Iron making spread from western Asia to Europe in the 12th century BCE. Iron Age Europe was home to a group of people called the Celts.

Iron Age sword

Celtic dagger in its case

Celts

The Celts settled in central Europe by 500 BCE. They then conquered large parts of Spain, France, and Britain. They made metal items out of iron, instead of bronze.

Forts

In Britain, the Celts built forts – towns on a hill that were surrounded by huge banks of earth and wooden fences. These forts made sure the houses were well guarded, as the Celts could see enemies coming from afar.

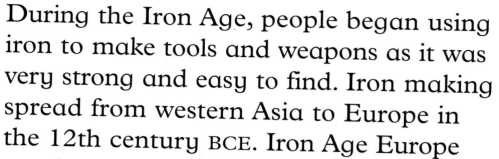

Families lived in round houses with straw roofs. These homes had one large round room with a fire in the middle, which was used for cooking.

Why are Celtic bodies from bogs so well preserved?

How was iron made?

Iron is a metal found in a type of rock known as an ore. In the Iron Age, people discovered how to extract the metal from the ores by heating them for several hours in a furnace. The result was a lump of iron that could be hammered into shape.

Ironworker

Furnace used to heat iron ore

When the iron from the furnace is hot, an ironworker hammers it to make a tool or weapon.

Beliefs

Celtic priests were called druids. They believed in many gods, and may have offered human sacrifices to them. This may explain why we have found human bodies from the Iron Age in bogs (wet and muddy lands) in Europe.

This silver bowl shows the druid ritual of sacrificing a bull.

Bronze horse harness decoration

Red glass was added to make an attractive pattern.

Decorative arts

People of the Iron Age made beautiful metal jewellery and decorative items, such as bronze ornaments. These were sometimes attached to a horse's harness.

Celtic warriors

The Celts were skilled and fearless warriors. The famous warrior queen Boudicca led her troops against the Romans in Britain in 60 CE. However, they were defeated, and the Romans took power of Britain.

An artist's impression of Boudicca and her followers

33

Routes

There were several routes along the Silk Road. These were difficult to travel across because of the very hot and dry weather. As well as bringing goods to Europe, merchants also traded between countries within Asia.

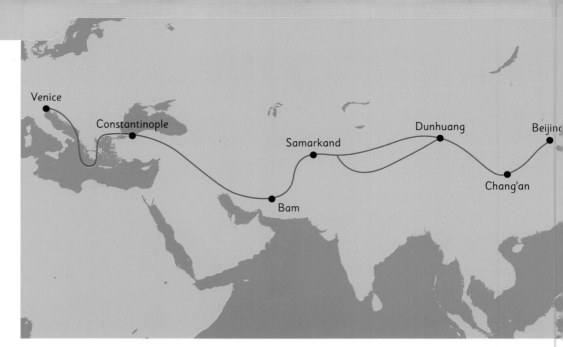

The Silk Road

From the 2nd century BCE, a series of land routes spread across Asia, linking China with Europe. Together, these made up the Silk Road. It allowed merchants to carry goods, such as silk and spices, to trade with Europe, where they were not produced.

Alexander the Great

By 331 BCE, this ruler had conquered many lands between Greece and modern-day Pakistan. He opened land routes in Central Asia that later became part of the Silk Road.

Travel

Due to the long distances, traders often stopped travelling when they reached a major market town. Here, they sold their goods to other merchants, who carried them on the next leg of the journey.

People rode the Silk Road on horses, while camels carried their goods.

How many years was the Silk Road used for?

Bam, a town in what is now southeastern Iran, was a part of the Silk Road.

Towns and markets

Towns on the road provided shelter for merchants to rest and marketplaces to trade their goods. Some, such as Bam, were also places where silk garments and other goods were made.

Silk

Only the Chinese knew how to make silk, so it was highly valued in Europe. This meant traders could charge expensive prices for it, making the long, hard journey worthwhile.

Cinnamon

Nutmeg

Spices

Many spices came to Europe from Asia, including cinnamon, nutmeg, turmeric, ginger, and pepper. These were costly, and only the rich in Europe could afford them.

35

It is thought to have been used for more than 1,000 years.

Maya civilization

Between around 1000 BCE and 1600 CE, the Maya people lived in bustling cities and built pyramids in Central America. Their beautiful books tell us about the ancient Maya world. The Maya still live in Mexico today.

Turn and learn
Aztecs
pp. 66–67
Inca Empire
pp. 68–69

Glyphs can be read like sentences.

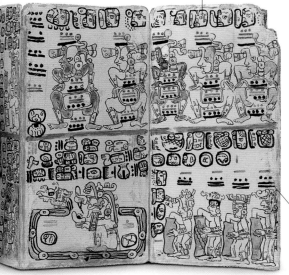

Writing
The Maya created a writing system that used symbols called glyphs. Each glyph stood for a whole word or part of a word. Groups of bars and dots showed numbers.

Maya numbers used a dot to show one and a bar to show five.

El Castillo is a pyramid in the ancient city of Chichén Itzá.

Priests performed rituals inside the temple at the top.

Pyramids
The biggest Maya buildings were stone pyramids. They had steep flights of steps to a temple at the top. Some were more than 70 m (230 ft) tall. The blocks of the pyramid took a long time to carve using tools made of stone.

Why was it important to win a Maya ball game?

Calendars

The Maya used the path of the Sun and Moon across the sky to make several different calendars. These showed months and years. The Maya even worked out when the Moon would move in front of the Sun in an eclipse.

Stone calendar plate

Glyphs showing 19 months sit around the edge of the Haab calendar.

Ball game

The Maya played a fast-paced game using a rubber ball and no hands! The aim was for players to use their hips to hit the ball through rings on the side of a court.

Chilli powder

Iguana

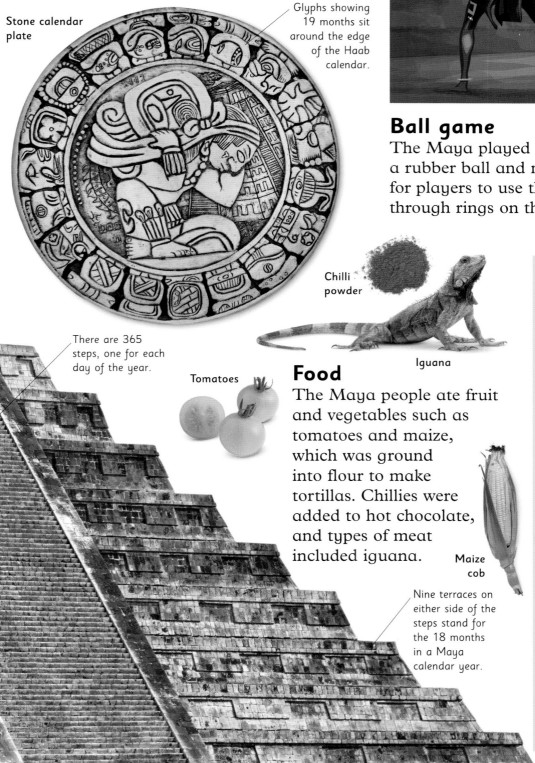

There are 365 steps, one for each day of the year.

Tomatoes

Food

The Maya people ate fruit and vegetables such as tomatoes and maize, which was ground into flour to make tortillas. Chillies were added to hot chocolate, and types of meat included iguana.

Maize cob

Nine terraces on either side of the steps stand for the 18 months in a Maya calendar year.

The Nazca

In South America, different civilizations lived at the same time as the Maya. The Nazca people in Peru lasted from around 100 BCE to 750 CE. They made giant pictures in the Nazca desert by moving rocks to show paler soil beneath.

This Nazca pottery head has an animal headdress.

The losing side could be put to death as a sacrifice to the gods!

Polynesian settlers

Polynesia contains more than 1,000 islands scattered across a huge area of the Pacific Ocean. Polynesian settlers were expert sailors and navigators, who planned expeditions to find new homelands. They settled all of their islands by 1300. By this time, the Polynesians were the most spread-out population on Earth.

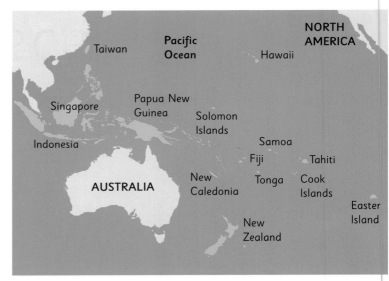

This map shows the islands settled by the Polynesians

Navigating
The Polynesians learned to navigate between the islands by watching the stars, ocean waves, and other signs. They made maps out of sticks, which showed currents and routes between the different islands.

This stick chart shows the routes between the islands.

How many people could a Polynesian canoe carry?

Maori mask from Rotorua in New Zealand

What did they take with them?

Settlers took animals with them, to make sure that they had a supply of food. They also took seeds that were used to plant crops on different islands.

Pigs were an important source of meat for the settlers.

Rats arrived with the settlers, having hidden in their canoes.

The taro plant was one of the main crops. The Polynesians ate its roots.

Polynesian fishing spear

Boats

People sailed in canoes that were made out of tree trunks. Many of these vessels had two main bodies, or hulls, to keep them afloat in rough seas. Smaller canoes were used for fishing in shallow waters.

Model of a Polynesian canoe with two hulls

Maoris

Polynesian settlers who reached New Zealand in the 13th century were known as the Maori. Isolated for centuries, they developed their own arts and crafts, such as making ceremonial masks.

Moai are said to represent great chiefs from Easter Island's history.

Easter Island

Easter Island was one of the last islands that Polynesian settlers arrived at. It is an isolated island in east Polynesia. Settlers built huge stone statues here, known as *Moai*.

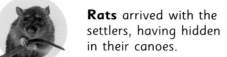

A canoe with two hulls could transport up to 50 people.

World religions

Most of the religions that people all over the world follow have existed for thousands of years. They mostly started with the teachings of great religious leaders in different places, before spreading across the globe.

This map shows the places where the major faiths were first followed.

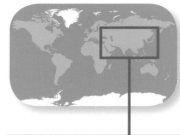

Islam

The Islamic faith was first spread by the Prophet Muhammad, known to Muslims as the messenger of God, in the early 7th century CE. Muslims worship a single God called Allah.

Christianity

In the 1st century CE, Jesus Christ, a Jewish teacher, was killed by being nailed to a cross by the Romans. After his death, his followers spread his teachings around the Roman Empire. Christians believe that Jesus was the son of God.

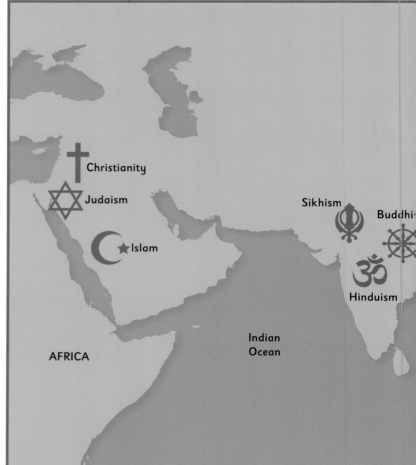

Christianity
Judaism
Islam
Sikhism
Buddhi...
Hinduism
Indian Ocean
AFRICA

A crucifix shows Jesus nailed to a cross. It is a symbol of Christianity.

Judaism

The ancient religion of Judaism was the first religion to worship only one God. Judaism led to both Christianity and Islam. The Jewish holy book is called the Torah.

The Western Wall in Israel is part of a Jewish temple built in the 1st century BCE.

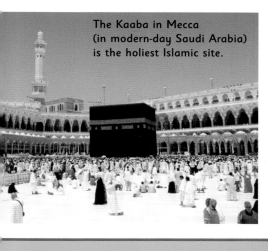

The Kaaba in Mecca (in modern-day Saudi Arabia) is the holiest Islamic site.

Statue of Hindu god Ganesh, the elephant god

Hinduism

Hinduism, the ancient religion of India, has no single founder. Hindus worship lots of different gods, and early sacred texts date back to around 1200 BCE.

Guru Nanak, founder of Sikhism

Sikhism

Beginning with the teachings of Guru Nanak in India in the 15th century CE, Sikhism is the youngest of the great world religions. Sikhs worship one God.

ASIA

Taoism

Pacific Ocean

Taoism

The Chinese faith of Taoism is based on a book called the *Tao Te Ching*, thought to be written by an ancient Chinese teacher called Laozi. Taoists aim to live their lives in harmony with nature.

Buddhism

Buddhists follow the teachings of the Buddha, who lived in northern India in the 5th century BCE. Buddhists do not worship gods – their goal is to achieve true wisdom by meditating, which involves thinking deeply.

Statue of the Buddha

Taoist pagoda (a type of tall building) in China

Anglo-Saxons

Soon after the Romans lost control of Britain in 410, Angles, Saxons, and Jutes from mainland Europe invaded Britain. The invaders eventually united the land under one ruler, forming their own Anglo-Saxon language and culture. They were conquered in 1066.

Did you know?
The Old English language used by Anglo-Saxons originally came from German and Danish invaders. Before this, the Britons spoke a Celtic language, which survives today as Welsh.

Kingdoms
Anglo-Saxon England was originally made up of around seven kingdoms, from Northumbria in the north to Wessex and Kent in the south. They were often at war with one another.

This is a copy of a finely made helmet belonging to a king, found in Suffolk.

Helmet from Sutton Hoo

Alfred the Great
Alfred (871–899), king of Wessex, fought off Viking invaders that had conquered a large area of Britain. Later kings of Wessex united the whole country.

This statue of King Alfred was made in 1899 to mark 1,000 years since his death.

Gold writing around the edge translates as "Alfred had me made".

The gold and enamel "Alfred Jewel" may have been a pointer used to follow text.

Which Old English letters are missing from the English alphabet?

Weapons

Most Anglo-Saxon warriors carried spears or axes and protected themselves with round shields. The sword was a weapon of upper-class men and military leaders.

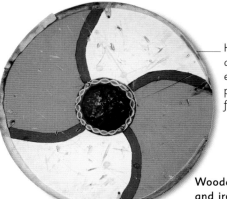

Hide (toughened animal skin) edging helped to protect shields from damage.

Wooden shield and iron sword

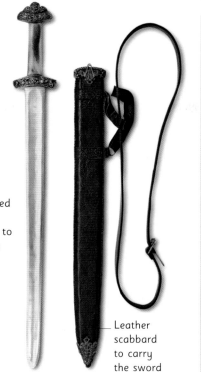

Leather scabbard to carry the sword

Bede, monk of Jarrow

Language and literacy

Priests and monks (such as the author Bede of Jarrow) were highly educated. They wrote in both Latin and the local language, now called Old English.

Crafts

The Anglo-Saxons loved patterns. They crafted beautiful jewellery, accessories, and vessels (containers). They used materials such as glass to make these precious items. Some glass was remade from Roman glass.

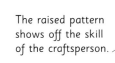

The raised pattern shows off the skill of the craftsperson.

Blue glass vessel

Christianity

In the 6th and 7th centuries, Christians came from Ireland and Rome to convert the Anglo-Saxons to their faith. The newly converted people built churches for worshipping in, as well as monasteries for monks to live and work in.

This church was built in the 7th century at Brixworth in Northamptonshire.

These carvings show figures from the Bible, the book of Christian teachings.

The cross is a symbol of Christianity. This is a piece of the 8th-century Rothbury Cross.

Vikings

The Vikings were people who lived between the 8th and 11th centuries CE. They came from Scandinavian countries like Norway and Denmark. The Vikings were skilled sailors who travelled far and wide in search of riches and new lands to conquer and live in.

The single large sail was made of wool or linen.

Turn and learn

Dwellings
pp. 54–55

Longships
The Vikings used longships to travel across the world. The ships were fast and had narrow bodies, which meant that they could travel up rivers as well as across oceans and seas.

Iron helmet with noseguard

Longships had rows of oars, which allowed the Vikings to travel quickly even when there was no wind to push the ship forwards by its sail.

Viking warrior

Warriors and raiders
The Vikings were fierce warriors who carried out raids on coastal villages and monasteries (religious buildings). They stole valuable items and took people as slaves.

Axes and spears were the Vikings' favourite weapons – both had iron heads.

Why did the Vikings invade other peoples' lands?

Brooch

Metalwork

The Vikings were highly skilled metalworkers. They worked with iron, bronze, silver, and gold to create jewellery and weapons.

Hammers were used to beat metal into shape.

Viking metalworker

Norse gods

The Vikings worshipped many gods. Each god was in charge of different parts of life and nature.

 Odin was the king of the gods. He controlled death and knowledge.

 Thor was the god of thunder and strength, and a protector of humankind.

 Loki was the shape-changing trickster god who caused accidents.

 Freyja was the goddess of love, beauty, and children.

Viking homes

Many houses had walls made from wood and roofs made out of straw. These were called longhouses, as they were made up of just one long room.

The longhouse was waterproof as it had a straw roof.

Shields were lined up along the side of the boat for protection.

Parents, children, workers, and animals lived together in longhouses.

Normans

The Normans were Vikings who settled in Normandy in northern France in 911 CE. They made a deal with the king of France, who allowed them to live there in return for protecting his people from attacks by other raiders.

The Bayeux Tapestry shows a Norman army crossing the English Channel to invade Britain in 1066, led by William the Conqueror.

They wanted to steal valuable items or to find new land to farm.

Medieval Europe

In the medieval period (about 1000–1500), much of Europe was controlled by a few powerful people. These were either kings or senior churchmen. It was a time of brilliant art and beautiful buildings. However, tiring farmwork was the only job open to most poor people.

A crosier is an ornate staff, or stick, carried by a bishop (church leader).

Church
People went to church often. Unlike most people at this time, monks and priests (who led church services) could read and write. This meant they could also work in government and gain lots of power.

Bishop's crosier

Knights wore metal armour into battle.

Flexible chainmail was made from thousands of tiny metal links.

Knights and castles
A knight led a group of men who would fight for the king in times of war. Knights had servants and farmers working for them and lived in large houses or castles.

People looked ou[t] enemies from tow[ers] and fired arrows [from] narrow windows [that] protected them f[rom] return arrows.

Bodiam Castle, UK

Why was medieval life so hard for the poor?

Village life

Most people lived in the countryside and worked in the fields. Farmers grew crops both for themselves and for their lord. They used only simple hand tools, and had to work long hours with few days off.

Cart for transporting grapes

This medieval French painting shows people harvesting grapes, which were used to make wine.

Feudal system

The king was head of society, and everyone had to obey him, from lords and knights to craftworkers and farmers.

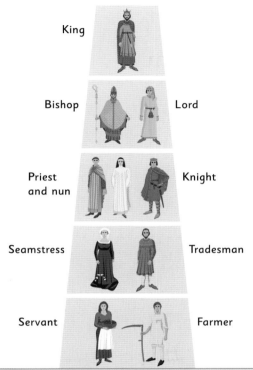

King

Bishop — Lord

Priest and nun — Knight

Seamstress — Tradesman

Servant — Farmer

Medieval women

There weren't many jobs available to ordinary women and girls, but they could be nuns or crafts-people such as seamstresses (whose job was sewing). At home, they often cooked, made clothes, and spun wool to make thread.

Embroidery was skilled work that took many hours.

Seamstress

Buildings

Huge cathedrals were built in major cities for Christians to worship inside. These had pointed arches and were decorated with beautiful stonework, statues of saints, and stained glass windows.

Tall spires were designed to look like they were reaching for heaven (the Christian afterlife).

13th-century cathedral in Coutances, France

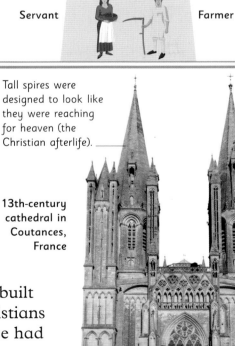

They had to do whatever their lord or king told them!

Byzantine Empire

The Greek-speaking eastern half of the Roman Empire survived after the western half ended in the 5th century. We call this the Byzantine Empire, after its capital Byzantium (now Istanbul, Turkey). Its law system is the basis of many laws today. It lasted about 1,000 years, despite often being at war.

Emperors Constantine (right) and Justinian (left) stand on either side of the Christian figures of Mary and Jesus.

Great leaders

The empire's capital was renamed Constantinople after Emperor Constantine, who made Christianity legal. Another famous leader, Justinian, rewrote many Roman laws.

Domed buildings

The Byzantines were brilliant at building impressive domes, which they used as roofs for many of their biggest churches. The insides often glittered with gold-speckled mosaics.

Hagia Sophia was the largest church in the world. People came from all over the empire to visit it.

This dome was one of the biggest in the world when it was completed in 537.

Who originally built the city of Byzantium?

Saints and Christians

Constantinople was a centre of Orthodox Christianity. Followers of this branch of the Christian Church use painted or carved images of Jesus and the saints to focus their thoughts and prayers during worship.

Jesus's mother, Mary, stands on his right. St John is on his left.

Tenth-century ivory (tusk) panels showing Jesus's crucifixion (death on the cross)

Strong towers and gates were built along the walls.

The double walls of the old city are still standing today.

Trade

The empire grew rich from buying and selling goods such as silk (from countries to the east) and grain. It used coins made of pure gold, which kept their value for centuries.

Gold coins

The minarets (towers) were added later, when the building became a mosque (Muslim place of worship).

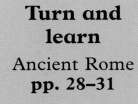

Turn and learn
Ancient Rome
pp. 28–31

Constantinople's walls

In the 5th century, Emperor Theodosius II built some of the strongest walls ever constructed around a city. These kept out the many armies that tried to invade the capital.

Fall of the empire

From the 13th century, the Ottoman Turks from Anatolia (now a large area of Turkey) took over some of the empire's eastern lands. They finally conquered Constantinople in 1453, bringing the Byzantine Empire to an end.

Ottoman troops under their leader Mehmed II broke through a section of the walls to capture the city.

The ancient Greeks built the city in around the 7th century BCE.

The Black Death

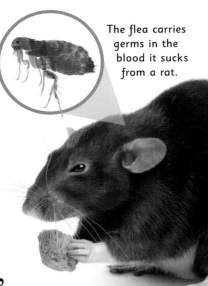

The flea carries germs in the blood it sucks from a rat.

A terrible disease called the Black Death killed millions of people in Europe and Asia during the mid-14th century. It was given this name because of the black swellings sufferers got on their skin. The Black Death was a very infectious (easily spread) disease, but no one knew what caused it or how to treat it.

Many rats lived on ships, so could carry diseases over long distances.

Bubonic plague

We now call the illness the bubonic plague. Before modern medicine, most people died a few days after catching the infection. The 14th-century outbreak wiped out whole towns and villages.

Monks often cared for the sick and tried to make them better. Sometimes they caught the disease from the sick.

Medieval doctors trying to treat the plague with medicine

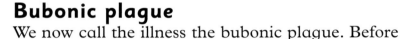

How many people were killed by the Black Death in medieval times?

How it spread

The Black Death swept quickly from Central Asia across Europe in 1347–1353. It was probably carried by fleas living on rats, although fleas may have also spread the disease from human to human.

These crosses were placed on the dead bodies of plague victims.

Lead cross

A bishop blesses a group of plague victims.

Treatments

Medieval doctors used mostly herbal medicines and "bloodletting" – removing blood from a patient. Neither of these treatments worked, but eventually they discovered that if a patient's swellings burst on their own, this was a sign that they might recover.

Wormwood was sometimes used in herbal remedies. Feverfew helped to calm fevers.

Feverfew

A fleam is an instrument with sharp blades for bloodletting.

Wormwood

Medieval beliefs

Since they could not understand the cause of the Black Death, many people believed it was God's punishment for their sins. They prayed to be spared from it, and priests blessed sufferers and their families.

People mourn as a victim is lowered into a grave.

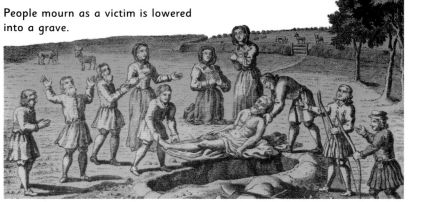

Later plagues

The Black Death ended in the 14th century, just as suddenly as it began. However, there have been other outbreaks since, including major ones in the 17th and 19th centuries. Today, the plague can be treated with medicines.

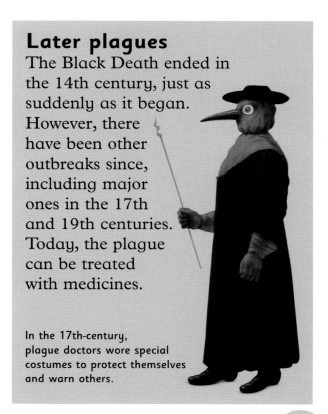

In the 17th-century, plague doctors wore special costumes to protect themselves and warn others.

Burying the bodies

People had to be buried quickly, often many at a time. Sometimes the bodies were buried together in pits to save time, because people were dying faster than coffins could be made.

Early Islamic civilizations

In the 7th century, Muhammad founded the religion of Islam. Soon after this, Muslim leaders conquered large parts of the world and converted most of the people living in these areas to Islam. These early Islamic civilizations have left behind beautiful buildings, books, and pottery.

The figure on this gold coin represents the Umayyad caliph Abd al-Malik ibn Marwan.

The first caliphs
Early Islamic leaders were called caliphs. The caliphs of the Umayyad period (661–750), the first Islamic dynasty, managed to extend their empire across western Asia and North Africa.

Islamic astrolabe, a navigational device that used the position of stars in the sky to guide travellers

Medicine
Islamic medicine was the most advanced in the world. It drew on knowledge gathered by other ancient civilizations, as well as Muslim doctors' own experience. The books of doctors such as Ibn Sina were famous and used for centuries afterwards.

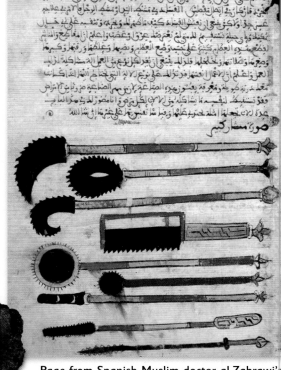

Exploration
There were many important Muslim travellers and explorers. They improved navigational equipment and journeyed far beyond the Islamic world. The explorer Ibn Battuta travelled to southeast and southern Asia, and even China.

These sal ammoniac crystals, and other naturally occuring minerals, were used by Islamic doctors in medicines.

Page from Spanish Muslim doctor al-Zahrawi's book *On Surgery and Instruments* (1000 CE)

How did Harun al-Rashid become famous outside the Islamic empire?

Harun al-Rashid

One of the most well-known caliphs of the Abbasid period was Harun al-Rashid (786–809). He built many new buildings in Baghdad, such as the House of Wisdom, which was considered the centre of learning in the city. He also encouraged scholars, artists, and musicians to come to the city.

Painting showing a young Harun al-Rashid

Baghdad

Under the Abbasid dynasty (750–1258), Baghdad became the capital of the Islamic empire. It was soon a large city and a centre of arts, crafts, and trade. Many scholars and teachers lived there.

Scholars in the House of Wisdom, Baghdad

The Great Mosque of Córdoba, Spain

Muslim Spain

The Muslims conquered Spain in the 8th century and stayed for hundreds of years. Their mosque in Córdoba and the palace of the Alhambra in Granada are among Spain's most beautiful buildings.

He is a character in the book of stories *The Thousand and One Nights.*

Mongols

The Mongols were a group of people who came from the grasslands of East Asia in the 13th century. They formed a huge army, led by Genghis Khan. The Mongols fought their way from Asia to Europe, conquering the lands along the way. They created one of the biggest empires in history.

Genghis Khan
The Mongol leader Temujin became Genghis Khan, or "ruler of the Mongols", in 1206. He wanted to conquer the world, and was a fierce warrior who led his army to many victories.

A giant 40 m (131 ft) high statue of Genghis Khan stands near Ulaanbaatar in Mongolia.

By using stirrups (footrests), the Mongols could control their horses with their legs. This left their hands free to use their bow and arrows.

Horsemanship
The Mongols were successful conquerors because they were skilled horsemen. They rode fast, covering large distances in a day, and their speed helped them win battles. They used special saddles that stopped them falling off their horses.

Why was the Mongol saddle so special?

Leather-clad armour and helmet

Bow used by the Mongols

Herding

The Mongols kept sheep and goats, which they herded from one area of grassland to another as they moved across Asia. These animals provided meat, milk, and wool.

Attack and defence

The Mongols' success in battle came from their speed and skill with the bow. They also wore armour made of metal plates, which protected them from sword strokes.

Helmet decorated with bronze

Mongol warrior's boots

Mongols in China

Genghis Khan captured Zhongdu (modern-day Beijing) in 1214. A later Mongol leader, Kublai Khan, took over the vast empire of China in 1279. His dynasty ruled China until 1368.

Dwellings

The Mongols moved around a lot so they lived in round tents called *gers*, which could be put up and taken down quickly and easily. Each *ger* had space for a whole family to live in.

The *ger* has a framework of thin wooden strips and is covered by warm, woollen felt.

Turn and learn

Viking homes pp. 44–45

55

Imperial China

By the 10th century, China had grown into a huge empire, ruled by a series of emperors and their families (called dynasties). The Tang Dynasty (618–907) welcomed ideas from other countries, which helped develop art and technology. During the Song Dynasty (960–1269), the population doubled.

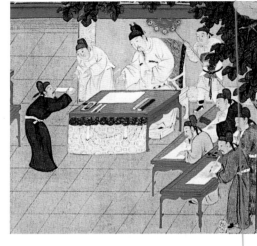

Running the empire
A huge country was hard for one person to rule, so each emperor had thousands of civil servants (government workers) to help. People had to pass a tough examination to do this job.

The *Diamond Sutra*, a Buddhist text translated into Chinese in 868, is the world's oldest surviving printed book.

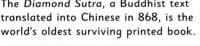

Literature
All kinds of literature (written works) developed under the emperors of the Tang Dynasty (618–907), especially poetry, fiction, and religious writing.

Ceramic burial horse from the Tang Dynasty, with red paint and carved decorations

Ceramics
The Tang Dynasty was known for its beautiful pottery. Ceramic figures were often made to be buried with people when they died as they were believed to help people in the afterlife.

56

Wu Zetian

Empress Wu (690–705) became the first and only female emperor of China. She was a strong ruler and promoted Buddhism, building many monasteries.

By 1014, bronze magnetic compasses, like this one, were used for navigation.

Technology

Chinese inventions were often developed far ahead of those in other countries. The Chinese invented gunpowder, clockwork, and the magnetic compass long before they were known in Europe.

Ming Dynasty

The emperors of the Ming Dynasty (1368–1644) strengthened the Great Wall of China, built a new capital at Beijing, and sent ships to explore other countries.

The painted dragon symbolizes the emperor and his family.

Ming-Dynasty porcelain bowl. Porcelain, a form of very fine pottery, was first made in China and sold all over the world.

Temple of Heaven, in Beijing, is one of the largest temples in China and was built in the Ming period.

57

Because her husband became ill and he could not rule any more.

Imperial Japan

The Edo period in Japan (1603–1868) was named after the capital city Edo, which is now Tokyo. During this time, Japan was run by a series of powerful men called shoguns. Japanese arts, crafts, and literature developed during the Edo period.

The shogun

The emperor was the head of the country, but the shogun ran it on his behalf. The shoguns led the army, controlled trade, and had power over the whole country. In the Edo period, the shoguns all came from one family, the Tokugawa family.

Tokugawa Ieyasu, the first Tokugawa shogun

Samurai warriors

Each area of Japan had its own military lord, who had high-ranking warriors called samurai. Samurai were highly skilled swordsmen and trained in military tactics. They promised to serve their lord, be brave in battle, and live an honest life.

Samurai armour was highly decorated, often made from many pieces of iron laced together.

Samurai katana (long sword), one of two swords often worn by warriors

This sword stand includes the badge of the Tokugawa family.

Why was the emperor considered to be special?

Rice

Rice was an important part of the diet in Edo Japan. It could grow well in Japan's mountainous areas, and farmers could make a good living selling the crop in towns and cities.

Rice plant

Theatre

The Japanese created a unique kind of theatre called *Noh* (meaning "skill"). *Noh* combines colourful costumes, masks, music, and movement to tell dramatic stories. It was enjoyed mostly by the upper classes.

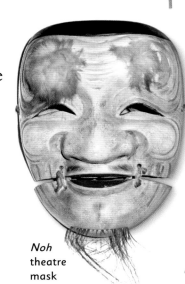

Noh theatre mask

Emperor Meiji (1852–1912) became ruler at age 15. He encouraged more trade with the West and helped to modernize Japan's culture.

Printmaking

People loved to display art in their homes, and many bought colourful prints. Prints were not as expensive as paintings, and artists such as Hiroshige made Japanese printmaking some of the best in the world.

Floating world

The rich people in the city of Edo had plenty of spare time to be entertained. They enjoyed music, theatre, and beautiful paintings, as well as wearing fine silk clothes. These pleasures were referred to as *ukiyo*, which means "floating world".

18th-century kimono, made of lightweight embroidered silk for hot weather

Meiji Restoration

In 1868, Japanese rule was restored to emperors after more than 250 years of rule by the shoguns. This was known as the Meiji Restoration, after the ruler of the time, Emperor Meiji. This period saw the modernization of Japanese society.

The Japanese believed that he was a living god.

Korea in the Middle Ages

From the 7th century, Korea grew as a centre of trade and the arts, first during the Silla period (57 BCE–935 CE) and then under the Goryeo (935–1392). Korea's most successful period was the Joseon (1392–1897), when advances in education and science were made.

Sejong the Great

The Joseon emperor Sejong (1418–50) defeated many pirates, made Korea's laws more strict, and improved trade with Japan. His scientists gathered knowledge about different farming methods, which allowed people to grow more food.

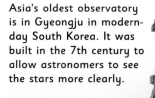

Asia's oldest observatory is in Gyeongju in modern-day South Korea. It was built in the 7th century to allow astronomers to see the stars more clearly.

Science and technology

Many new discoveries and inventions were made during the Joseon period. These included more accurate calendars, equipment for telling the time, a new way of measuring rainfall, and models of the Solar System.

Why was the Hangul alphabet so much easier than Chinese for Koreans to use?

Medicine

Korean doctors used herbs and acupuncture (putting needles into points on the patient's body) to treat people. They created new medicines and improved the ways nurses cared for sick people. By the Joseon period, more than 50,000 medicines were available.

Korean goods

Korean potters made many fine pots, especially celadon ware, which had a pale green glaze. It was sold abroad, which brought a large amount of wealth into the country.

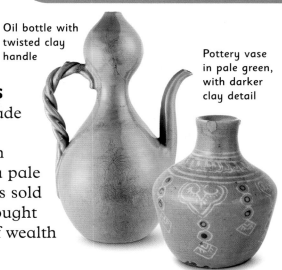

Oil bottle with twisted clay handle

Pottery vase in pale green, with darker clay detail

This giant statue in Seoul, South Korea, shows Sejong the Great holding a book in the Korean alphabet that he created.

Wooden printing blocks, each used to print one page of a book

Printing

The Koreans were the first people in the world to use printing. At first, they printed from wooden blocks with letters hand-carved into them. Later, they developed metal printing, with each piece of metal containing one letter.

Wooden printing block with Hangul script

People wrote with a brush using solid ink that they mixed with water.

Writing

Originally, Koreans used the Chinese writing system to write their language. In around 1443, however, Sejong created Hangul, a simpler way of writing Korean. This meant that many more people could learn to read and write.

Korean writing desk with stamps

Because it has only 24 letters, whereas Chinese uses thousands of characters.

African kingdoms

Throughout history, many separate kingdoms have existed in the huge continent of Africa. Some of these were extremely rich. Many of them traded, or swapped, goods with distant lands. The kingdoms contained skilled craft workers, large cities, and complex religions.

Rulers of Benin

Benin was based in West Africa's rainforests. By the 15th century, it was a powerful empire under rulers called Obas. They conquered their neighbours and traded with countries as far away as Portugal.

This bronze head probably shows Idia, the powerful mother of 16th-century Oba Esigie.

The leopard was a symbol of the Oba's power, since in the wild it is known for its strength.

Trade

When European merchant ships started to call at West African ports in the 1400s, the Benin people traded with them. They swapped goods such as ivory (or tusks) and even slaves for items from Portuguese traders.

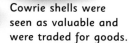

Cowrie shells were seen as valuable and were traded for goods.

Ivory was used to make figures such as this one, which may show a princess from Benin.

When did the kingdom of Benin end?

People taught and studied at universities such as the Djinguereber Mosque in Timbuktu.

Mansa Musa

A Muslim ruler of Mali in the 14th century, Mansa Musa was fabulously rich. He went on a pilgrimage, or religious journey, to Mecca and built schools when he returned.

Musa holds a nugget of gold in this 14th-century drawing.

Empire of Mali

Mali in West Africa was a powerful kingdom in the 12th and 13th centuries. Gold from the land and items such as books were traded for other goods, such as salt. This made people very rich. Scholars and students filled the city of Timbuktu.

Mali had more gold than almost anywhere else on the Earth.

Zimbabwe

By the 13th century, the people of the Zimbabwe plateau in southern Africa were sending gold and copper to be sold in Asia. They built large settlements at home with big stone walls.

Mansa Musa spent so much gold on his pilgrimage that tales of his riches reached Europe.

The walled settlement of Great Zimbabwe was a bustling city between the 11th and 15th centuries.

The kingdom was defeated and taken over by the British in 1897.

Indigenous people of North America

When European settlers arrived in North America in the 15th century, it was home to hundreds of nations. We call such people indigenous, which means belonging to a place. They lived by hunting in some areas, while in others they farmed.

Nations are said to live in 10 "cultural areas", each with a similar way of life.

Arctic
Subarctic
Northwest Coast
Northwest Plateau
Great Basin
Great Plains
Northeast
California
Southeast
Southwest

Indigenous lands

The landscapes and climates of North America are very different – from the freezing Arctic in the north to hot southwestern deserts. Indigenous people used local materials for their homes, clothes, and tools. They hunted local animals and gathered plants for their food.

Model of a kayak. Kayaks were made from sealskin on a whalebone or wooden frame.

The far north

The Inuit nations of the Arctic lived by fishing and hunting animals such as reindeer and seals. They made kayaks (a type of boat), clothes, and huts out of waterproof animal hides (skins). Snow was used to make homes called igloos.

How many indigenous people live in the USA today, in 2019?

Traditional crafts

Some nations carved totem poles (huge wooden posts shaped like animals or humans). Animal skins were made into beautiful leather items. Beads were often used to make jewellery or to decorate clothing.

Glass beads were traded from settlers.

Indigenous warriors carried leather shields.

Pueblo revolt

In the Southwest, many indigenous people lived in villages that 16th-century Spanish settlers called *pueblos*. The Spanish and indigenous people often fought. In 1680, a force of men from *pueblos* revolted (rose up) against the Spanish, chasing them from the area.

Wars with settlers

Nations often tried to stop settlers from taking over the lands they lived on. In the mid-19th century, the Lakota and other nations joined forces to fight against the US Army in battles on the Great Plains.

Buffalo skin tepees (tents) could be put up in an hour.

Plains nations

The nations of the Great Plains hunted buffalo, which gave them meat, hides, and horns. They made houses, clothes, and tools out of the hides and horns. They often moved around on horseback or foot looking for buffalo.

The Lakota leader Sitting Bull led warriors to victory in the Battle of Little Bighorn in 1876.

Around 5.2 million indigenous people live in the USA.

Aztecs

From around 1320, people began to live and farm in the Valley of Mexico in Mexico. They made earth islands in the swampy land and farmed crops such as maize on top of them. On a large island in Lake Texcoco, they built a city that seemed to float on the water, called Tenochtitlan. Its people conquered nearby lands to form the Aztec civilization.

Stone knife used to sacrifice victims

Sacrifice to the gods

The Aztecs thought gods controlled the world. They killed people and animals as gifts to the gods so that they would provide things such as good harvests.

Gods

There were many Aztec gods that were thought to control different aspects of nature, such as the Sun or rain.

Quetzalcoatl took the form of a man or a snake. He created the world and controlled the wind.

Huitzilopochtli led the Aztecs to their first city, Tenochtitlan. He was also the god of war.

Tlaloc, the rain and water god, was important to Aztec farmers as his rain watered their crops.

Tenochtitlan

By the 15th century, Tenochtitlan had grown to house over 200,000 people. A huge pyramid-shaped temple stood in the centre. The city's remains now sit buried beneath Mexico City.

Temple for worshipping the rain and water god, Tlaloc

Gifts to the gods, such as human sacrifices, were carried up the staircases. The bodies of the sacrificed were then thrown down the steps.

The Great Temple towered over other buildings at around 60 m (140 ft) high, about the same as 14 double-decker buses.

What was an Aztec flower war?

Home life

Women did jobs such as teaching, but at home they prepared food, wove cloth, and cared for the family. Men usually worked in the fields, growing crops such as maize.

Most men had their hair cut to around chin-length. Women often wore their hair in two twists.

Warriors

All boys trained to be warriors. Warfare was important to the Aztecs for conquering nearby lands and taking prisoners that could be sacrificed to the gods.

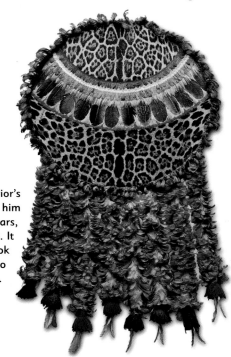

The Aztec warrior's shield protected him from enemy spears, swords, and clubs. It was made to look impressive so as to scare opponents.

Temple for Huitzilopochtli, god of war

Conquests

Spanish conquerors invaded Mexico in the 1520s, led by Hernán Cortés. They defeated the Aztecs by convincing people the Aztecs had conquered to fight with them. They also brought deadly diseases from Europe.

This picture shows the armoured Spanish marching towards Tenochtitlan. The bearded man at the front is Cortés.

A war to take prisoners who could be sacrificed to get a better harvest.

Society

Inca society was like a pyramid, with most people at the bottom and one very powerful emperor at the top.

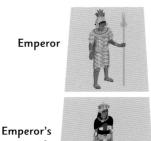
Emperor

Emperor's wife

Priests High priest

Lords Nobles

Farmers Servants

Inca Empire

From around 1200 to 1500, the Incas built a vast empire across the western side of South America. These people were expert farmers, had organized societies, and built impressive cities high up in the mountains.

Machu Picchu

This mountain-top city in Peru dates back to the 1400s. It is thought to have been built as a place for royal people to live.

Most Incas were farmers. They planted crops such as maize and potatoes along strips of land cut out of the slope like giant steps.

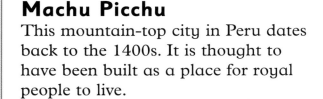

What was the total length of the Inca roads built across the empire?

Gold

Gold was sacred to the Incas. They made figurines as offerings to their gods, and emperors gave gifts of gold as rewards to soldiers.

Religion

Inca people worshipped many gods and believed each one was responsible for different aspects of life – from the weather to farming.

The god Viracocha was thought to be the creator of the world.

Gold llama used as a religious offering

Clay plate used in religious worship

The Incas built houses with blocks of stone and nothing to stick them together. The blocks' weight and the way they fitted together held them in place.

Recording information

Incas used groups of knotted threads called *quipus* to keep track of information. They used knots to stand for different numbers, so that they could record taxes, population figures, or dates.

A *quipu* was created from threads made of llama wool.

The roads stretched across around 24,000 km (15,000 miles).

Age of exploration

Between 1450 and 1800, explorers set sail to cross oceans and find new lands to conquer. This period is known as the age of exploration. Most of these explorers were European, and they had new types of ships and navigation tools that allowed them to make long sea voyages.

Trade

Explorers discovered places where expensive items could be found cheaply. Spices from Asia, such as nutmeg and pepper, and metals from Africa and America, such as gold and silver, were traded by merchants all over the world.

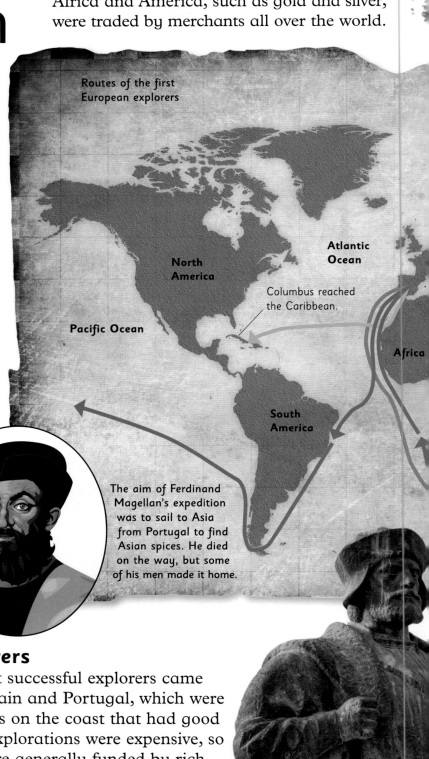

Routes of the first European explorers

North America

Atlantic Ocean

Columbus reached the Caribbean.

Pacific Ocean

Africa

South America

The aim of Ferdinand Magellan's expedition was to sail to Asia from Portugal to find Asian spices. He died on the way, but some of his men made it home.

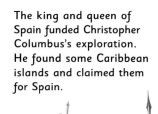

The king and queen of Spain funded Christopher Columbus's exploration. He found some Caribbean islands and claimed them for Spain.

Explorers

The first successful explorers came from Spain and Portugal, which were countries on the coast that had good ships. Explorations were expensive, so they were generally funded by rich people, such as European rulers, who hoped to find lands to conquer.

What did Columbus hope to gain from his voyage?

Peppercorns

Nutmeg

Gold nugget

Pirates

Pirates were a big danger to sailors, as they went to sea and robbed other ships. Some explorers were pirates themselves, and attacked their rivals' vessels to steal the trade goods they were carrying.

Gold and silver goods were the most prized treasure for pirates.

Some pirate ships flew a skull and crossbones flag in the hope of scaring other sailors.

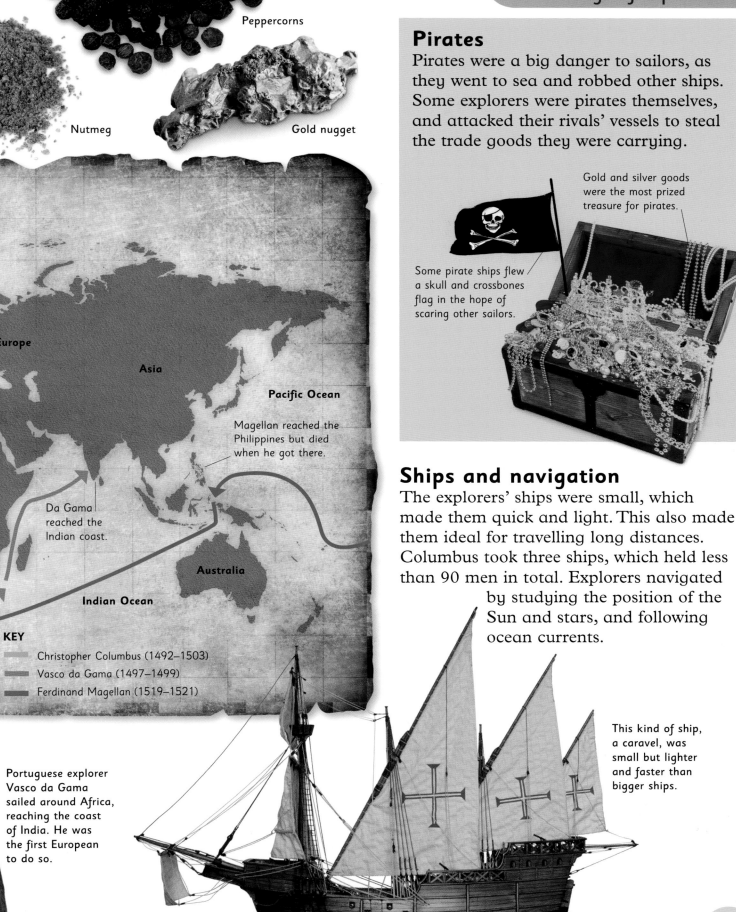

Europe

Asia

Pacific Ocean

Magellan reached the Philippines but died when he got there.

Da Gama reached the Indian coast.

Australia

Indian Ocean

KEY

Christopher Columbus (1492–1503)
Vasco da Gama (1497–1499)
Ferdinand Magellan (1519–1521)

Ships and navigation

The explorers' ships were small, which made them quick and light. This also made them ideal for travelling long distances. Columbus took three ships, which held less than 90 men in total. Explorers navigated by studying the position of the Sun and stars, and following ocean currents.

This kind of ship, a caravel, was small but lighter and faster than bigger ships.

Portuguese explorer Vasco da Gama sailed around Africa, reaching the coast of India. He was the first European to do so.

71

The king and queen of Spain promised to make him ruler of the lands he discovered.

European colonies

North American areas containing French (shaded pink), Spanish (shaded blue), and British (shaded yellow) colonies in around 1721.

From the 15th century, Europeans began to settle in the areas they reached during voyages of exploration. Goods such as food were sent from these colonies (areas ruled from abroad) to be sold in Europe. African people were sold as slaves too.

Central and South America

The Spanish and Portuguese wanted the precious metals silver and gold from this region, as well as crops such as sugar and coffee. They forced locals to farm crops and mine (dig up) metals.

North America

Valuable goods for trade attracted several European countries to North America. French people in Canada gathered furs, the British on the East Coast grew crops such as tobacco, and the Spanish in the South made locals farm crops for them.

Spaniard Francisco Pizarro conquered the Incas and took control of Peru. After this, many Spanish people moved there.

The Spanish used South American silver to make coins and ornate objects such as this censer (incense burner).

Why did so many local people die under the colonists' rule?

The pilgrims

Colonists celebrated Thanksgiving (their first harvest) with the locals who had helped them.

Many English settlers came to North America in 1620 when their way of worshipping was banned. These "pilgrims" (religious travellers) were helped by locals to grow North American crops for food.

India

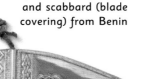

Knife with gold handle and scabbard (blade covering) from Benin

The British set up the East India Company in 1600 to trade spices in Indonesia and cotton in India. Soon, large numbers of British people began to settle in India. Britain used its army to control government leaders and rule the country through them.

The East India Company made its own coins with the approval of the British ruler.

Batavia was controlled by the powerful Dutch East India Company. They had their own army and warships.

Cloves

Cinnamon

Africa

From the 15th century, Europeans were selling Africans as slaves (people owned by others). Most of Africa had been colonized by seven European countries by the end of the 19th century. Objects made by African craftspeople were also sold. These were made from valuable materials such as gold and ivory.

Ivory (tusk) ornament from Benin

Indonesia

Both the English and the Dutch wanted to sell the spices of the Maluku Islands (or Moluccas) in Indonesia. These included cinnamon and cloves. The Dutch were more successful. They set up their own trading town, Batavia (now Jakarta), on the coast of Java in Indonesia.

Many died from overwork, cruel treatment, or from diseases brought by colonists.

The Slave Trade

From the late 15th to the 19th centuries, European traders bought slaves in Africa and sold them to people, such as farmers, in the Americas. Slaves had no freedom, meaning they were their owner's property. They were treated badly, did hard work for long hours, and often died young.

Transport

Slaves were packed together so closely in traders' ships that they could hardly move. They travelled in pain and discomfort from Africa to the Americas. Many slaves died on the journey.

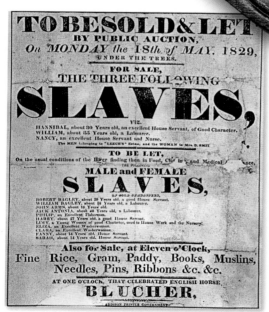

Poster advertising a slave sale in the USA

Slave market

African slaves were sold to the public at auctions (a sale where people offered money to buy them). Around 7 million slaves were sold in this way before the Slave Trade ended in the 19th century.

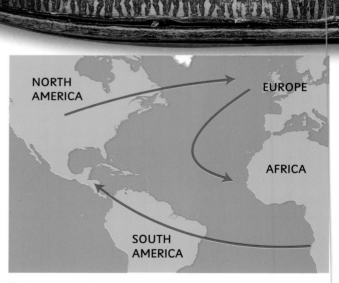

Triangular trade map

Traders took goods, such as cloth, from Europe to Africa, in exchange for African slaves. They then took the slaves to the Americas to sell for crops. These crops were taken back to Europe to sell to factories. This process was called triangular trade.

74

Whip used to punish slaves

Life of a slave

Slaves worked very hard and faced cruel punishments if they disobeyed their masters. The usual punishment was whipping or beating, and some slaves who tried to escape were beaten so badly that they died.

Iron shackles (cuffs) were sometimes put on slaves' legs to stop them escaping.

This model of a slave ship shows how slaves were crammed together with no space to move. Some ships carried as many as 600 slaves.

A 19th-century cotton plantation with slaves working in the fields.

Abolition

Many people hated slavery. They produced objects, such as this medal, to encourage the abolition, or ending, of slavery. The Slave Trade was banned by Britain in 1807, but it still continued in other places.

Plantations

Many slaves worked on plantations, which were large farms. Plantation owners grew crops, such as cotton or sugar cane. Slaves had to work long hours in the hot sun and had very few breaks.

Slaves were freed in the USA in 1865, but slavery still continues in some modern countries.

The Renaissance

From around the 14th to the 16th centuries, people in Europe began to rediscover the art and writings of ancient Greece and Rome. This knowledge helped them form new scientific ideas and create beautiful artworks. We now call this time the Renaissance (rebirth).

Italian beginnings

The Renaissance began in the Italian city-states, such as Florence and Rome. Artists such as Michelangelo began to paint and sculpt clear, lifelike figures. They were especially interested in re-creating people as they really looked.

Turn and learn
Ancient Greece
pp. 22–25
Ancient Rome
pp. 28–31

The Marriage of Arnolfini, by Jan van Eyck from Flanders (now part of Belgium), uses oil paints to show how light enters a room.

Michelangelo's *Pietà*, a marble sculpture of the dead Jesus held by his mother

Northern Renaissance

The Renaissance spread northwards to areas such as England, Germany, and the Netherlands, where education and scholarship (specialist study) grew popular. Their artists often created portraits (pictures of people) and religious works in oil paint.

What do people mean when they call someone a Renaissance man or woman?

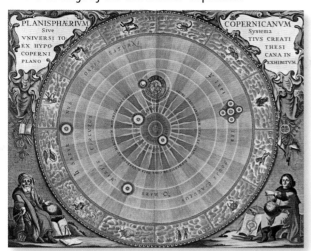

17th-century picture of the Solar System, based on the writings of the astronomer Copernicus

New kinds of music

Renaissance musicians wrote lots of instrumental music. This was played at dances or at home. Instruments included the lute, which is plucked like a guitar. Complicated renaissance choir music was written to be beautifully sung by a group.

This lute was made in Venice in around 1500.

Science

Renaissance scientists based their work on evidence, such as what they saw. For example, when astronomer Nicolaus Copernicus looked at the planets, he realized that they moved around the Sun, and not around the Earth as people had thought before.

People learned how to successfully treat many diseases for the first time during the Renaissance. These painted pottery containers held medicines.

The Roman-style dome of Florence Cathedral was designed by Filippo Brunelleschi and completed in 1436.

Domes and columns

Many Italian cities were transformed during the Renaissance. Builders copied ancient Roman and Greek building styles. They added Greek-style columns as well as structures that the Romans used, such as domes.

A person who can master any skill and whose knowledge of every subject is very wide.

The Reformation

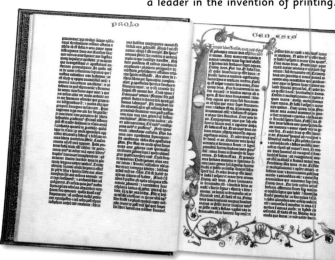

This Bible was made by Johannes Gutenberg, a German inventor. He was a leader in the invention of printing.

In 16th-century Europe, many people were unhappy with the way the Catholic Church was being run. Some of these people, known as Protestants, wanted to make changes within the Church, while others went on to form new, Protestant Churches. This was called the Reformation.

Printing

Protestants wanted to read the Bible, but most were unable to as it was written in Latin, a language that many could not understand. The invention of printing made it quick and easy to create Bibles in many languages, such as German and English.

Leaders

Across Europe, the Reformation's leaders fought for change against the practices of the Catholic Church.

Martin Luther, one of the first reformers, translated the Bible into German.

John Calvin came from France. He spread Protestant teachings in both France and Switzerland.

Ulrich Zwingli was from Switzerland, and also had followers in other parts of Europe.

The Gutenberg printing press was invented in around 1439. It pushed a sheet of paper onto inky metal letters to print words.

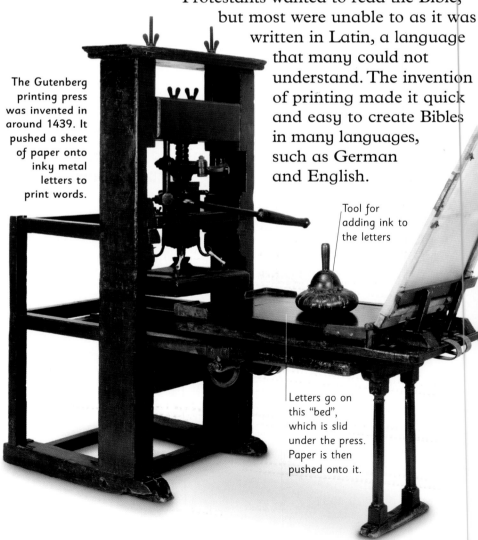

Tool for adding ink to the letters

Letters go on this "bed", which is slid under the press. Paper is then pushed onto it.

Which European countries stayed strongly Protestant after the religious wars?

The English Reformation

King Henry VIII wanted to divorce his first wife, which the Catholic Church did not allow. The king decided that England should stop following the Pope (the Catholic leader). He closed down Catholic monasteries and founded the Church of England, which was later made Protestant.

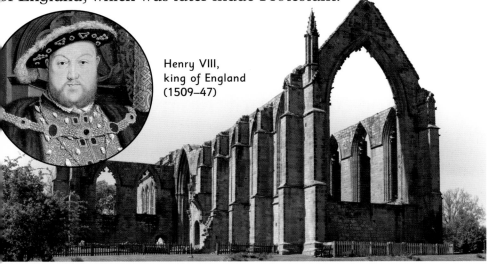

Henry VIII, king of England (1509–47)

Bolton Abbey in Yorkshire, England, became damaged and fell into ruin after Henry VIII closed it.

Large statues of saints, such as this one of Saint Theresa in Rome, Italy, encouraged commitment to the Catholic Church.

The Catholic response

The Counter-Reformation was a movement by the Catholic Church to defend their teachings. Measures included punishing people who didn't obey Church rules, and a new style of Christian art.

Fire of London

In 1666, many of London's buildings were destroyed by a terrible fire. A lot of people wrongly thought that the fire was started by Catholics attacking people because of their Protestant beliefs.

Religious wars

Sometimes arguments between the Catholics and the Protestants became violent. Wars broke out between the two sides all over Europe in the 16th and 17th centuries. Many people died during these religious wars.

In 1572, the Catholic French king ordered Protestant leaders to be killed. Thousands more Protestants died, in what is known as the St Bartholomew's Day Massacre.

Switzerland, Scotland, England, Sweden, Denmark, and much of Germany.

Ottoman Empire

Osman I (1299–1323) founded the Ottoman Empire in modern-day Turkey in 1299. By 1500, the empire was huge. It had spread from what is now Iraq to eastern parts of Europe and to northern Africa. The empire lasted until 1922.

The Ottoman army used curved swords.

Sword sheath with gold decoration

Sultans

The rulers of the Ottoman Empire were called sultans. They lived in luxury and had lots of power. Many were also leaders of the army. All of the sultans of the Ottoman Empire were from the same family.

Army

The Ottoman army was large and organized, and helped conquer new lands. A group called the Janissaries, who were the sultan's slaves, were the most well-trained soldiers.

Razor-sharp blade

Did you know?

From 1453, the city of Constantinople was the capital of the Ottoman Empire. The Ottomans called the city Istanbul, the name still used in Turkey today.

Suleiman I (1520–66) was a sultan who led the empire when it was at its largest and most powerful.

How did the Ottoman Empire get its name?

Sultan Ahmed built this mosque in Istanbul between 1609 and 1616. It can hold 10,000 people, and is called the Blue Mosque because of the blue tiled walls inside.

Forts

The Ottomans built forts (buildings with protective walls around them) outside their main cities. The strongest forts were outside Constantinople (modern-day Istanbul). They had stone walls and towers from where defenders of the city could shoot at approaching enemies.

The Rumeli Hisari Fortress in Istanbul

Islam

The sultans were Muslims. They built large, beautiful mosques (Muslim places of worship) and ruled using religious laws. Many of their people became Muslims, but the Ottomans let people practise other religions, such as Judaism or Christianity.

Christian forces defeat the Ottomans at Lepanto.

Arts and decoration

Some Muslim artists made pottery in the town of Iznik, in modern-day Turkey. They painted patterns of flowers on objects, and used popular colours such as green and blue. Artists also decorated the tiles used on the insides of buildings.

Iznik plate, made in the 17th century

Battle of Lepanto

To stop the Ottomans from conquering more of Europe, Pope Pius V (the head of the Roman Catholic Church) brought together a group of Christian nations. In 1571, the Ottomans were defeated by the Christian forces at the Battle of Lepanto, off the coast of Greece.

It was named after Osman I, the first Ottoman sultan.

Mughal Empire

The Mughals were Muslims from Central Asia who conquered India in 1526 and built an empire that lasted for more than three centuries. During this time, they made advances in science, and created impressive architecture and beautiful works of art.

Painting of the Battle of Panipat (1526)

The Mughal conquest

Babur became the first emperor of the Mughal Empire after he invaded northern India in 1526. He defeated the sultan of Delhi at the Battle of Panipat, marking the beginning of the Mughal Empire.

Akbar the Great

The Mughal emperor Akbar (1556–1605) expanded the empire to cover almost all of the Indian subcontinent. He treated people of all religious backgrounds equally, and married a Hindu princess. Akbar also loved and encouraged the arts.

Miniature painting of Emperor Akbar

Brass globes showing the stars in the night sky were often used as decorative objects but also as a guide for astronomers

Astronomy

Under the Mughal emperors, Muslim astronomers and Hindu scientists worked together to produce some of the period's best research into the Sun and the stars.

At what age did Akbar become emperor?

Mughal army officer carrying a rifle

A *Divan* (collection of poems) from the Mughal Empire

Water jug made of carved green jade

Gunpowder

Babur learned about guns and how to use them in battle from Ottoman experts. The use of firearms allowed his soldiers to defeat much bigger armies that did not have such powerful weapons.

Mughal arts

The arts, from metalworking to carving, developed under the Mughals. They especially liked beautifully illustrated books. Artists were influenced by styles from Persia, painting detailed, colourful images of people, animals, and flowers.

Architecture

Mughal architecture was at its finest in the 17th century, when Emperor Shah Jahan built the Taj Mahal to house the tomb of his wife, Mumtaz Mahal. Around 20,000 workers helped build the stunning building.

The walls of the Taj Mahal are made of carved and decorated marble.

Emperor Akbar came to the throne at only 13 years old, after his father died.

Settlers in Australasia

European explorers landed in Australia in the 17th century when they were searching the Pacific Ocean for southern lands. In 1788, the British started their first colony in Australia, and a colony in New Zealand was created soon after.

Specimen (sample) of a plant called *Banksia*. It was named after botanist Joseph Banks, who travelled with Captain Cook.

Captain Cook

In 1770, British explorer Captain James Cook sailed to the South Pacific. He landed in New Zealand and continued on to Australia, where he drew maps of the east coast, watched wildlife, and met the local people. Captain Cook made two more Pacific trips, and explored the ocean further.

Captain Cook is holding a rolled-up map. He was a skilled mapmaker.

Iron shackles (cuffs) were used to stop British prisoners from escaping on the journey to Australia. Some were attached to a heavy iron ball.

Statue of Captain Cook in Alaska, USA

Port Jackson

The first British settlement in Australia was founded at Port Jackson, Sydney, in 1788. It was a penal colony (a place where prisoners are sent to live). Many prisoners then got married and had children in Australia.

How many prisoners did the British send to Australia?

Time of change
The arrival of Europeans changed the lives of the indigenous people of Australia (Aborigines) and New Zealand (Maoris). Many were forced off the lands that they had lived in and travelled through for thousands of years. Lots of people died from diseases brought by the settlers.

New Zealand
By the early 19th century, there were several European settlements in New Zealand. Some of the Maori people learned new farming methods from the European settlers, but others clashed with them.

Poster advertising a ship sailing to New Zealand

Traditional Maori club (a weapon) made from jade (a type of hard, green stone)

Wooden Aborigine boomerang used for hunting

Gold rush
Gold was discovered in Australia in the 19th century. In 1851, a large amount of gold was found in southeast Australia. People rushed there from Britain, Ireland, the USA, Germany, and China. They tried to make a fortune by searching for the valuable metal.

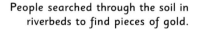
People searched through the soil in riverbeds to find pieces of gold.

The British and the Maoris
The British government set up an official colony for British settlers in New Zealand in 1840. An agreement, called the Treaty of Waitangi, was made between the British and the Maoris. This gave the British the power to rule New Zealand. It removed the Maoris' right to rule, but allowed them to keep their lands.

The British settlers and the Maoris sign the Treaty of Waitangi in 1840.

About 162,000, before the system ended in 1868.

American Revolution

In the early 1770s, the British ruled 13 areas, called colonies, in North America. In 1775, the colonies started a war with their British rulers, as they wanted to rule themselves. They won the war in 1781, and they created an independent country called the United States of America.

Statue of George Washington, the first president of the USA in Boston, USA

Boston Tea Party
Some of the money that the colonies spent on tea was taken by Britain as a tax. A group of Americans decided to protest against the British tax in 1773, and boarded British tea ships in Boston Harbor to throw all of the tea into the sea in protest.

George Washington
When Britain said it was going to punish the American tea protesters, George Washington (a politician) became leader of the American army against the British. Washington was later made the first president of the USA.

Did women or children take part in the fighting?

Brown musket (gun) that was used by the British forces

Turning point

The turning point of the war came in 1777, when the colonial army beat the British at Saratoga, New York. This victory convinced France to join America's side, and the final British surrender came in 1781.

British leaders surrender to the Americans after the Battle of Saratoga, 1777

Tricorn hats were worn by members of the American colonial army.

Life on the home front

The battles of the American Revolution were close to people's homes. Many people heard the fighting and helped the wounded soldiers by cooking them meals and mending their uniforms.

Women sewing one of the first American flags

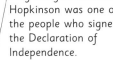

Declaration of Independence

The leaders of the 13 colonies signed a document called the Declaration of Independence on 4 July, 1776. It said that America should be independent and free from British rule.

Flag designer Francis Hopkinson was one of the people who signed the Declaration of Independence.

The stars and stripes

The first US flag had 13 stars and 13 stripes, to represent the original colonies that became the first 13 states. As more states were added to the USA, the number of stars was increased.

The opening words of the Declaration of Independence

Many boys joined the army, while some women pretended to be men to join.

French Revolution

Between 1789 and 1799, a huge revolution happened in France. A group of people removed the king and Church from power and turned France into a republic (a country whose leaders are chosen by the people). They wanted to make sure that all French people had equal rights (opportunities) and freedom.

The king

The French king, Louis XVI, lived in luxury in his palace in Versailles, near Paris. He had total control over the country. Other members of the royal family and Church also had money and lived an easy life.

Storming the Bastille

The king did not help the poor people of France. An angry crowd broke into the prison at Bastille, Paris, and released the prisoners. The violent removal of the king had begun.

Revolutionaries attacked the Bastille prison on 14 July, 1789.

The people

After recent wars, most of the people in France were left in poverty. There were shortages of food, such as bread, and they had to pay high taxes to the royals, which made people very poor.

Why did the revolutionaries need to reduce the power of the Church?

The revolutionary forces

Most of those who fought for the people of France were from the lower classes of French society. They were known as the revolutionaries. They wanted a better life and believed that fighting was their only option.

The Tricolor cockade was the badge of the revolutionaries. It was blue, white, and red.

Turn and learn

American Revolution pp. 86–87

Revolutionaries were called *sans-culottes*, or "people without breeches" (a type of trousers). They wore loose trousers instead of the tight, knee-length breeches worn by the upper classes.

Portrait of a French revolutionary fighter in around 1789

Queen Marie Antoinette was executed in 1793.

The Terror

After four years of fighting, the new French government had not achieved peace. Those in power became cruel, and began a reign of terror. People who opposed the government were killed using the guillotine (a device with a sharp blade that falls to chop off a head).

Liberty, equality, fraternity

The revolutionaries fought to gain liberty, equality, and fraternity. These mean freedom, equal rights for all, and brotherhood. These words still form the motto of the Republic of France.

New coins were issued without the king's portrait on them.

The new French flag was based on the colours of the Tricolor cockade.

Napoleon

Napoleon Bonaparte was a military commander who was an important member of the French government during the revolution. He became dictator (ruler with complete power) of France and then emperor. This meant that France was again ruled by one person.

Napoleon Bonaparte, French general and emperor

The Church collected taxes from the people and had huge influence over their lives.

Industrial Revolution

Puffing Billy is an early steam engine. It was built in 1813.

In the 18th and 19th centuries, new machines were introduced in factories around the world. These were powered by water or steam, and could make items faster than by hand. This huge change was called the Industrial Revolution, and it affected the way millions of people lived and worked.

Cities

Thousands of people moved to towns and cities to work in factories. Working indoors in noisy conditions, and living in cramped cities, was a big shock to many people. They were used to the open air and space of the countryside.

Most workers lived in small houses, with no gardens or running water.

Rows of mechanical looms weave cloth in a large factory.

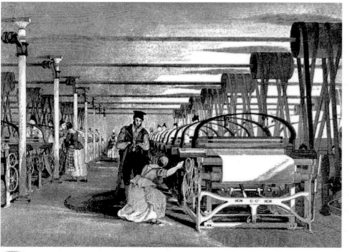

Factories

Many of the first factories made cloth using looms, which were powered by steam. Looms could weave material much faster than a person. The work in these factories was hard as the hours were long. Early machinery could also be dangerous to use.

90

Steam engines

During the Industrial Revolution, engines were powered by steam. These steam engines were first used to pump water out of mines. They were later attached to wheels and used to pull trains along tracks to transport goods and passengers.

The world's first iron bridge was built by iron manufacturer Abraham Darby in 1779. It stands over the River Severn in Shropshire, UK.

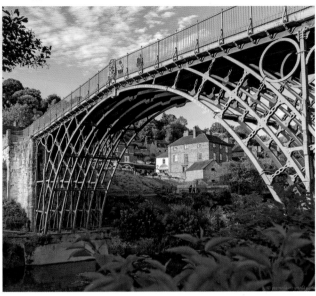

Trains with steam engines carried coal to factories.

Canal boats were used to transport goods from factories to shops.

Coal and iron

Coal was needed not just to power steam engines but also to make iron. Coal-powered furnaces heated iron so that it would be soft enough to mould into shape. Iron could then be used in many new ways, such as building factories, bridges, and machines.

Small children had to push heavy carts of coal along narrow tunnels in the mine.

Child labour

Many children did hard, dangerous work in factories and mines. Children were used as workers because they could be paid less than adults. However, some people in government tried to ban very young workers so they could go to school instead.

Many people, even children, worked for 16 hours a day.

Imperial world

Throughout the 18th and 19th centuries, European countries traded with the rest of the world more and more. They colonized, or took over, some of the countries they traded with, and became rulers of the colonies. Some countries, such as Britain and France, had large worldwide empires, and became known as imperial powers.

Warren Hastings, the first British governor of Bengal, India

Effects of imperialism
European rulers forced many people in their colonies to work in tough and dangerous conditions. They were often made to follow European traditions and religions.

Turn and learn

Imperial China **pp. 56–57**
Imperial Japan **pp. 58–59**

Imperial rule
Britain fought a war in the 18th century to gain control of Bengal, India. They chose a governor, who ruled Bengal and other parts of India. He governed either with the help of local rulers or by reducing the power of the local rulers.

During the Indian Mutiny in 1857, Indians fought against their British rulers.

How did the imperial powers benefit from ruling other countries?

The Great Trek
In 19th-century South Africa, the Boers, a group of Dutch-speaking settlers, wanted to be free of British rule. Between 1835 and 1845, around 15,000 Boers left the British colony and travelled further into Africa. We now call their journey the Great Trek.

This painting shows the Boers on their journey northeast out of South Africa.

Leopards mounted on a person's head

The scramble for Africa
France, Britain, Belgium, and several other European countries colonized most of Africa in the late 19th century. There was a rush between them to be the first country to control places that had lots of gold, gems, and other valuable materials.

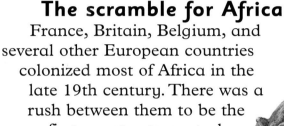

Mask made by the Yoruba people from Africa

War bonnet worn by a chief of the Lakota nation

During the land wars in the USA, indigenous warriors used knives, arrows, and guns, but were often outnumbered by settlers.

Cloth makers in Jabalpur, India

Land wars in the USA
In 1862, the US government gave land to European settlers in western USA. This forced indigenous (local) people to leave their homes, causing war to break out between indigenous nations, such as the Lakota nation, and European settlers.

Buying and selling cloth
Many Indian cloth-makers were put out of business under British rule. This was because British rulers taxed cloth that was produced in India. This made it very expensive to buy. The British then sold their own cheap cloth in India, to help British cloth factories make more money.

They could control supplies of goods like tea, cotton, and other items not found at home.

American Civil War

In 1861, a war broke out between the northern and southern states of the USA, who disagreed about slavery. The northern states wanted to end slavery in the USA and the southern states wanted to keep their slaves. In 1865, after around 700,000 people had died, the northern states won the war and the slaves were freed.

Confederate flag, known as the "stars and bars"

The Union side used the "stars and stripes" flag.

A statue of Lincoln stands in Washington, D.C., USA. Lincoln's fight to end slavery in his country made him a national hero.

Turn and learn
The Slave Trade
pp. 74–75

The two sides
The northern, or Union, states had many factories with paid workers. Many northern people thought slavery was wrong. In the southern, or Confederate, states, slaves were needed to work on the many plantations (large farms).

Abraham Lincoln
Lincoln became president of the USA in 1860. He wanted to end slavery and when it became clear that he was against it, the southern states started the war. Lincoln announced that all slaves would be freed when the war ended, but he was shot dead by a supporter of the South in 1865.

How did the Union weaken the Confederate army?

The Battle of Gettysburg
At first, the Confederates did well in the war, due to skilled army leadership. However, the Union had a bigger army, and scored important victories at battles such as Gettysburg in July 1863, where thousands died and the Confederates were forced to retreat.

Gettysburg was a major victory for the Union, and a turning point in the war.

Before the invention of radio, telegraphs could send messages along wires.

Bullets were wrapped up with gunpowder to give guns enough power to shoot them.

Modern war
The conflict is often called the first modern war. For the first time, electrical equipment such as the telegraph was used to send messages instantly. Soldiers also had better guns, and railways and iron ships could transport supplies and troops.

The Sharps Carbine was a reliable rifle much used in the war.

Union soldiers' hats were not worn for fighting, but for jobs such as cleaning.

"Wanted" poster advertising a reward for the capture of an escaped slave

100 DOLLARS REWARD!
Ranaway from the subscriber on the 27th of July, my Black Woman, named **EMILY,** Seventeen years of age, well grown, black color, has a whining voice. She took with her one dark calico and one blue and white dress, a red corded gingham bonnet, a white striped shawl and slippers. I will pay the above reward if taken near the Ohio river on the Kentucky side, or THREE HUNDRED DOLLARS, if taken in the State of Ohio, and delivered to me near Lewisburg, Mason County, Ky. THO'S. H. WILLIAMS. August 4, 1853.

Slaves during war
A lot of slaves were forced to work for southern armies, but many escaped to fight on the Union's side. They hoped to be free and to have the rights of other Americans, such as being able to own property.

End of the war
The surrender of the largest Confederate army by General Robert E. Lee in April 1865 gave the Union almost certain victory. The other Confederate armies soon surrendered. The slaves were freed after the war but many had to keep doing back-breaking farmwork.

By blocking Confederate ports so that merchant ships could not deliver supplies.

Archduke Ferdinand of Austria and his wife, Sophie, just before they were killed in 1914

Map of the Central Powers and the Allies in Europe

Ireland
Britain
Portugal
France
Germany
Austria-Hungary
Italy
Serbia
Greece
Romania
Bulgaria
Black Sea
Russia
Ottoman Empire
Morocco
Algeria
Mediterranean Sea

| | Allies | | Western Front |
| | Central Powers | | Eastern Front |

Global war

War broke out when a Serbian killed Franz Ferdinand, the heir to Austria-Hungary's empire. The allies of both countries, and their worldwide colonies, joined the war. It was fought along two fronts (lines).

World War I

The first world war (World War I) began in 1914 in Europe. Two groups of countries fought against each other until 1918, and many millions of people died during this time. The two sides were the Central Powers (including Austria-Hungary, Germany, and the Ottoman Empire) and the Allies (including Britain, Russia, and France).

Conscription

At the start of the war in Britain, people volunteered to fight, encouraged by posters such as this one. However, they were put off from fighting as more and more soldiers were killed, so the government started to force men to join the army. This is called conscription.

BRITONS "WANTS YOU"
JOIN YOUR COUNTRY'S ARMY!
GOD SAVE THE KING
Reproduced by permission of LONDON OPINION

Did the USA join the war?

British troops go into "no-man's land", which is the ground between the two sides' trenches.

The Somme
The Battle of the Somme, in northwest France, lasted 140 days. It was the deadliest battle in the war, as around one million soldiers were wounded or killed.

Trench life
While away at war, soldiers lived in trenches dug in the ground, which were only a short distance from similar trenches dug by the enemy. Battles were fought in the land between, both sides trying to capture the enemy's trench.

The conditions in the trenches were bad. They were damp, muddy, and cold.

Modern warfare
The two sides used lots of new inventions to help win the war. These also made the war very deadly and dangerous.

 Poison gas stopped victims from being able to breathe. Soldiers wore gas masks, which protected them.

 Aeroplanes were used for spying on the enemy, fighting, and dropping bombs.

 Tanks could crawl over obstacles on the battlefield and even over trenches.

Poppies are worn as a memory of soldiers who died in the war.

End of the war
The war ended with the victory of the Allies in 1918. A peace treaty (agreement) made the the Central Powers give up some of their land, and they had to pay huge fines to the Allies.

There are military cemeteries across Europe, such as this one in Ypres, Belgium.

They joined the Allies in 1917, when Germany sank some of their ships without warning.

Communism

During the 20th century, some countries became communist. In communism, property, such as housing and business, is owned by the whole community. The aim is for no one to be more important than anyone else. However, most communist countries failed to achieve this ideal.

Communist posters showed workers as heroes. The message on this Russian poster says: "We destroyed our enemy with weapons; we will earn our bread with labour!".

ОРУЖИЕМ МЫ ДО
ТРУДОМ МЫ ДО
ВСЕ ЗА РАБОТУ

The Russian Revolution

In 1917, poverty and hunger led people to violently overthrow the government in Russia. The royal family were removed from power, the aristocracy lost their land, and Russia became communist.

Russia's communist army, the Red Army, used a red star as its badge.

The USSR used machines such as this early tractor to modernize farming.

The USSR

Russia united in 1922 with smaller neighbouring countries, such as Ukraine, to form a huge new communist, or socialist, state. This was called the USSR (Union of Soviet Socialist Republics).

Why did people dislike communism if it treated people fairly?

The Iron Curtain

After World War II, many Eastern European countries, such as Poland, became communist. They worked closely with Russia, and used closed borders to cut themselves off from western Europe. We call this division between countries the Iron Curtain.

Joseph Stalin, leader of the USSR from 1922–53, punished critics of communism by sending them to work camps, prison, or to their death.

The Little Red Book by Chinese communist leader Mao Zedong

China

China became communist in 1949. Like Russia, it cut itself off from the non-communist world. Until the 1970s, people who disliked the regime were given poor jobs, put in prison, or killed.

Communism around the world

There are five communist countries that exist today, including China. Some, such as Cuba and Laos, were given money by the USSR to help them succeed in their early years.

This old Laos banknote shows the communist Pathet Lao forces fighting to overthrow the government, whom they eventually defeated.

The hammer and sickle (a farming tool) formed the most common communist symbol in Russia.

Monument to protests in Czechoslovakia (now Czech Republic and Slovakia) that led to the country's peaceful "Velvet Revolution" in 1989

Fall of Communism

In 1989, states in Europe began to get rid of communism. Most people hated a system where they often couldn't do or say what they wanted. Today's communist countries usually have little contact with the rest of the world.

There were often shortages of basic items, and punishments for those who complained.

Women and the vote

In the late 19th century, women had fewer rights than men, and could not vote in elections. Some women began to campaign, or fight, for suffrage (the right to vote). British campaigners included the suffragists, who protested peacefully, and the suffragettes, who took more direct action.

British suffragettes marching through London in 1908

Suffragettes

The suffragettes were a group of protesters, who campaigned for women's votes in Britain. Their motto was "Deeds, not words", so they took action, such as setting buildings on fire and breaking windows.

Under arrest

The suffragettes' actions often led to arrests, and many went on hunger strikes in prison. These methods rarely worked, and often had the opposite effect. Some people argued that women should not be given the right to vote because of their behaviour.

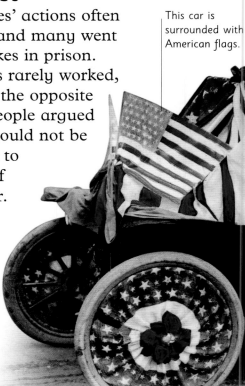

This car is surrounded with American flags.

British suffragette leader Emmeline Pankhurst was arrested outside Buckingham Palace, London, in 1914.

What reasons did men give for being against women's right to vote?

Key women

The suffrage movement had brilliant leaders in many parts of the world. Suffrage did not happen for most countries until well into the 20th century.

Kate Sheppard campaigned for the vote in New Zealand, succeeding in 1893.

Millicent Fawcett was one of the leaders of the British suffragists.

Susan B. Anthony was a well-known campaigner for the vote in the USA.

Effect of the war

Some men said that women were not their equals and so should not vote. During World War I, women worked in jobs that were previously done by men, such as factory work, and showed they could do these jobs just as well.

THE FRENCHWOMAN IN WAR-TIME

Poster showing women working in France during World War I

American suffrage pennant (banner)

VOTES FOR WOMEN

Worldwide suffrage

Throughout the 20th century, women in more and more countries won the vote. All British women could vote by 1928, but in Saudi Arabia women had to wait until 2015. Women in the USA won the right to vote by 1920.

Young women in a car at an American suffrage meeting in around 1920

VOTES FOR US — WHEN — WE ARE WOMEN

Young girls join in the protest for the women's right to vote.

The fight goes on

Today, women campaign for things such as equal pay, better conditions at work, and better education. The struggle for equal rights continues.

Two young girls at a protest for women's rights in Philadelphia, Pennsylvania, USA in 2017

They said that women were not as intelligent as men, and that women were too emotiona

The Great Depression

In 1929, many businesses and banks in the USA began to fail. As a result, millions of people lost their jobs. As more people became unemployed (jobless), there was less money to buy goods and even more businesses failed. The crisis soon spread worldwide and the Depression lasted around 10 years.

Wall Street Crash

Shares are portions of companies that people can buy and sell at stock exchanges, such as the one on Wall Street, New York City. Share prices suddenly plunged during the "Wall Street Crash" in 1929. Many people who had bought shares lost their money and the Depression began.

A man is forced to sell his car for money after losing all his savings in the Wall Street Crash.

$100 WILL BUY THIS CAR MUST HAVE CASH LOST ALL ON THE STOCK MARKET

Housing crisis

Many people bought their homes with loans (money lent from the bank or special companies). With no job, some could no longer pay their loans and lost their homes. Others became homeless when loan companies shut down.

Homeless people created "shanty towns" with houses made of odd pieces of wood. They had no heating or running water.

Why did people leave their farms in the Midwest USA?

Global Depression

The USA's problems spread. Countries such as Britain and Germany soon faced widespread unemployment and poverty. Many places did not recover fully, because a lot of factories and other big employers closed down.

JARROW PROTEST MARCH TO LONDON.

Protesters against poverty and unemployment in the UK marched 468 km (291 miles) from Jarrow to London in 1936.

Films helped spread the idea of the American Dream.

The American Dream

Many people in the USA believed in the American Dream. This is the idea that anyone could make their lives better if they worked hard and well. Many doubted that this was true after the Great Depression.

The New Deal

In 1933, President F.D. Roosevelt introduced the New Deal. This was a set of policies such as providing loans to farmers that didn't cost much to pay back, starting big building works to give people jobs, and helping the old and unemployed.

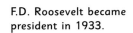

F.D. Roosevelt became president in 1933.

End of the Depression

The New Deal, and the hard work of those who had jobs building roads, dams, bridges, and power stations, improved life for many in the USA. When World War II came, many more found work making supplies for the armies.

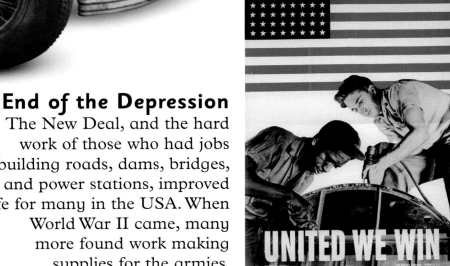

UNITED WE WIN

Poster encouraging people to work hard to support the war

Because drought and dust storms made their land impossible to grow crops on.

World War II in Europe

History's longest, most deadly war began in Europe, when Germany started to take over nearby countries. The fighting spread worldwide, lasting from 1939 to 1945. Widespread bombing from the air and tank-led land invasions made the war very destructive.

Europe, 1942

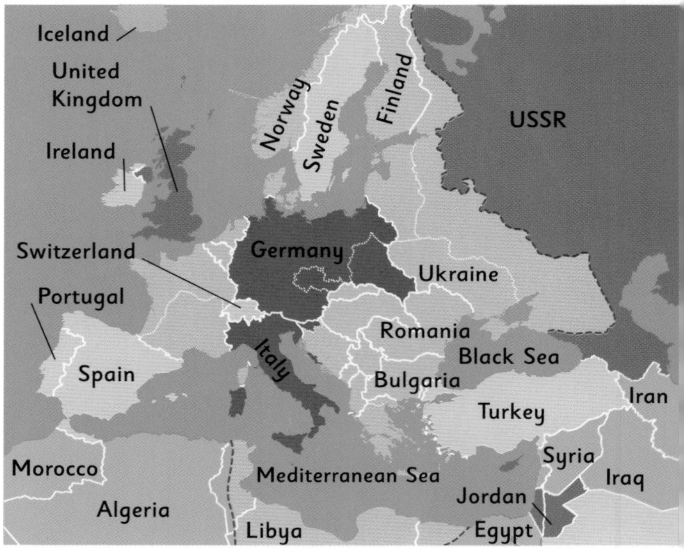
Iceland
United Kingdom
Ireland
Norway
Sweden
Finland
USSR
Switzerland
Germany
Ukraine
Portugal
Italy
Romania
Black Sea
Spain
Bulgaria
Turkey
Iran
Morocco
Mediterranean Sea
Syria
Iraq
Jordan
Algeria
Libya
Egypt
Allies
Axis
Controlled by Allies
Controlled by Axis
Neutral (didn't fight)
Front in Europe

Hitler and the Nazis

The head of the Nazi party (political group), Adolf Hitler, became leader of Germany in 1933. He soon took over neighbouring countries. Poland was invaded in 1939, so Britain and France declared war on Germany.

Allied and Axis powers

The European war was fought between the Allies (Britain and the USSR, now Russia) and the Axis powers (Germany and Italy). Each side controlled other countries.

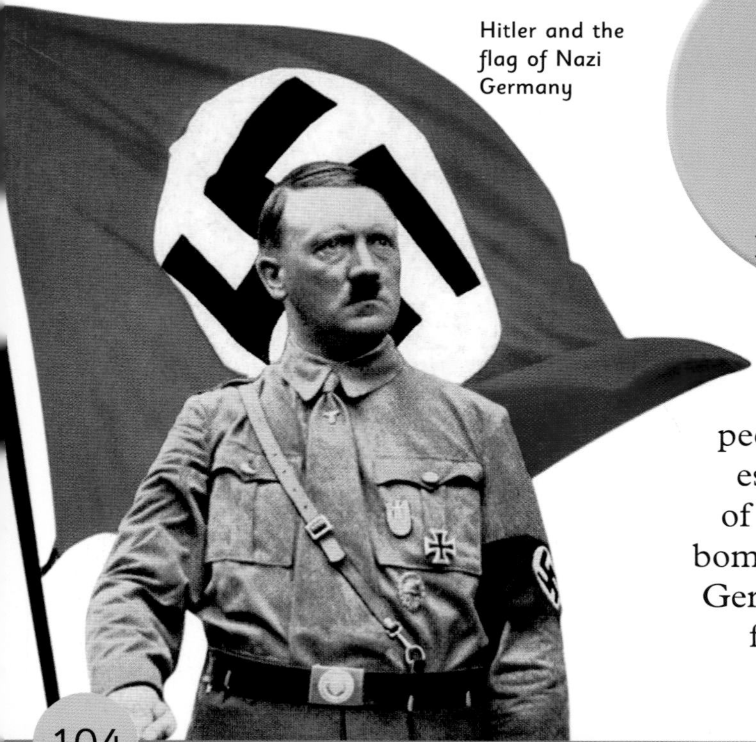

Hitler and the flag of Nazi Germany

Turn and learn
World War I **pp. 96–97**
Women and the vote **pp. 100–101**

War in the air

Bombing killed many people off the battlefield, especially in cities. Tens of thousands died in one bombing raid on Dresden, Germany. Power stations, factories, and railways were all destroyed.

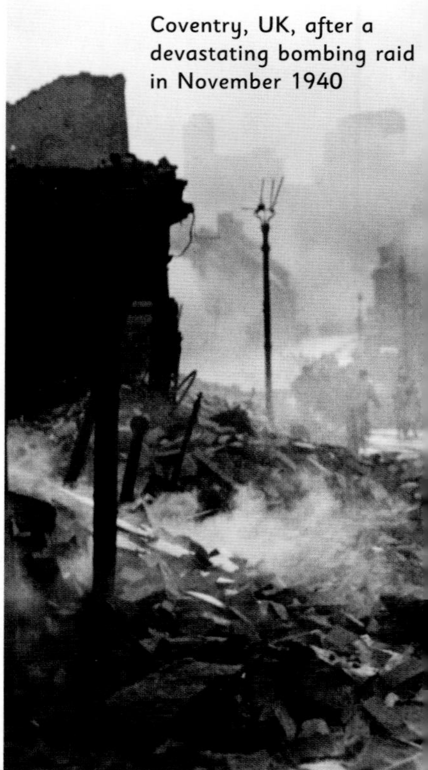

Coventry, UK, after a devastating bombing raid in November 1940

Why was there sometimes a shortage of food?

Posters encouraged women to help the war effort.

We Can Do It!

WAR PRODUCTION CO-ORDINATING COMMITTEE

Women at war

Some women joined the armed services in non-fighting roles, such as nursing. Women fought in the army of the USSR (now Russia). Many took on jobs at home. These included making things such as aircraft in factories or growing food to help with shortages.

Entrance to the Nazi concentration camp at Auschwitz, Poland

The Holocaust

The Nazis hated Jewish people. They rounded up Jews in conquered countries and sent them to work camps or death camps. Many were murdered in these places, as well in their hometowns.

Fighter aircraft such as Britain's Spitfire Mk 1 often shot bombers out of the sky.

The drone of a bomber plane such as Germany's Junkers Ju 88 was a scary sound.

Child evacuees

Bombing made cities unsafe, so many parents evacuated (sent away) their children to live in the countryside. These children had to live with strangers in unfamiliar places.

Evacuees with name labels

105

The wider war

The war spread further as it continued, with Japan and the USA joining in 1941. New technology began to play an important role. Early computers were used to break codes and nuclear bombs were invented. The Axis powers began to weaken in 1943. In 1945, the Allies won.

Code breakers

The countries at war sent messages to each other in complicated codes. The Allies used an early computer to break (work out) the Axis codes. The information they uncovered, such as plans of attack, helped win the war.

Words were typed into the machine for it to turn into code.

German Enigma machine, which made coded messages

Pearl Harbor was bombed on 7 December, 1941.

Pearl Harbor

In 1941, Axis power Japan sent aircraft to launch a surprise attack on the US base at Pearl Harbor, Hawaii. They seriously damaged 21 ships and killed 2,403 Americans. This brought the USA into the war on the Allied side.

Around 900 tanks were used in the battle, such as this German model.

The Battle of Stalingrad

The deadliest battle in history began in August 1943, between Axis armies and the USSR (now Russia). The USSR won after five months of fighting. Germany suffered a huge loss of soldiers.

106

Normandy landings

In June 1944, the Allies sent a huge army to land on the beaches of Normandy, France, which Germany had conquered. This was a big risk. However, they defeated German forces and pushed forward to gain areas of France, and then Germany.

US troops land in northern France on D-Day (the code name used for the day by the military), 6 June, 1944.

The Atomic bomb

The Allies won the war in Europe in May 1945. However, Japan fought on. To end the fighting, the USA dropped hugely powerful nuclear bombs on the Japanese cities of Hiroshima and Nagasaki in August, forcing Japan to surrender.

Nuremberg trials

The surviving Nazi leaders were put on trial from November 1945 to October 1946 at an international court in Nuremberg, Germany. Their harmful actions against innocent people led them to be found guilty of war crimes and crimes against humanity.

People accused of crimes at the Nuremberg trials

It gave the Allies territory in Europe from which to further attack the German army.

Independence

Many areas became independent from their 19th-century European rulers in the 20th century. However, different groups sometimes fought for power and new leaders weren't always very popular. In most of these areas today, people can vote for their leaders and everyone is treated equally.

Robert Mugabe was Zimbabwe's first president. He held onto power until 2017.

India and Pakistan

In 1947, India won independence from Britain after a long, peaceful campaign. It was split into India and what is now Pakistan and Bangladesh. Violence broke out between Hindus, who mainly lived in India, and Muslims, who mainly lived in Pakistan.

Africa

From Egypt in 1922 to Zimbabwe in 1980, African countries gradually took back control from their European rulers. In some cases, such as in Zimbabwe, a single politica party (group) took power and used force to stop people voting for other parties.

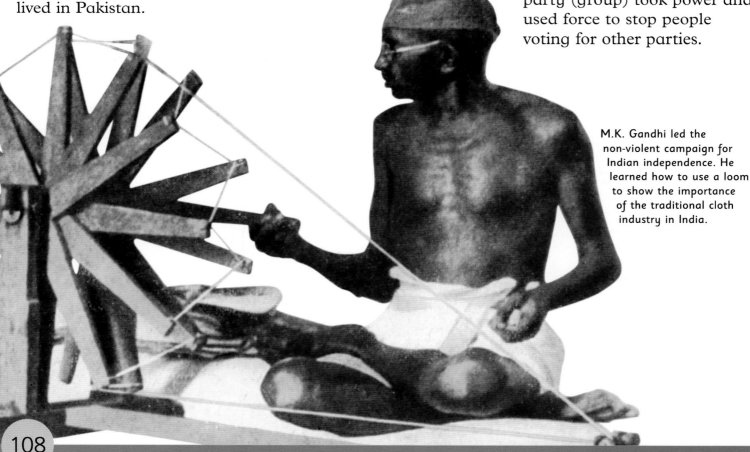

M.K. Gandhi led the non-violent campaign for Indian independence. He learned how to use a loom to show the importance of the traditional cloth industry in India.

108

Middle East

Many parts of this area were governed by France and Britain. When they became independent, there were tensions and sometimes wars between neighbouring areas. Jews in Israel and Muslims in Palestine continue to fight over land today.

British troops left Palestine in 1948, when the new Jewish state of Israel was founded.

The continuing struggle

Though most countries are free from foreign control, some still experience tensions with indigenous people (those who have lived there the longest). They are sometimes treated unfairly and have few or no representatives in the government.

The Inukshuk, a human-shaped statue made by the indigenous Inuit people of Canada, is used as a symbol of hope and friendship.

Turn and learn

European colonies **pp. 72–73**

Imperial world **pp. 92–93**

Oceania

Australia and New Zealand still have close ties to Britain, which once ruled them. Most of the smaller Pacific Islands have also become independent from Britain, Germany, and other rulers. They often have unique traditions.

Children in Fiji perform a traditional dance.

Yes – places such as Anguilla and Bermuda (British territories) and Guam (USA).

Civil rights

During the mid-20th century, black people in the USA and other countries faced discrimination (unfair treatment of a group of people). Many protested for black people to have the same civil rights (freedoms) as others. These campaigns pushed governments to make laws that protect black people, but there is still work to be done.

Segregated drinking fountains were clearly labelled

Segregation in the USA

The American policy of segregation meant that black people were not allowed to use the same facilities as white people, including schools and public toilets. They also had to sit at the back of the bus.

Key people

The Civil Rights Movement was led by brave people, who took risks to fight for equal rights for everyone.

Rosa Parks protested against segregation, and refused to give up her bus seat for a white person.

Martin Luther King Jr was an inspiring leader who encouraged non-violent protests.

Malcom X encouraged people to take direct action in the fight for civil rights.

110

How did the Civil Rights Movement affect children?

The Civil Rights Movement

In the 1950s, in the USA, people began to protest for black people to be treated the same as white people. The campaign promoted actions, such as speeches, marches, and boycotts (refusing to use segregated facilities).

Rosa Parks riding on a new, non-segregated bus

Marches

Many of the civil rights protests were non-violent marches, where people gathered and protested on the streets. During the March on Washington in 1963, Martin Luther King Jr gave his "I have a dream" speech. He spoke about a future USA, where everyone has equal rights.

Leaders of the March on Washington protested for equal jobs and freedom for everyone. Around 250,000 people attended this march.

African National Congress (ANC) flag

Apartheid

From 1948, in South Africa, there were apartheid ("separateness") laws. These forced black people to live in different areas from white people. They could only do jobs with low wages and they had very few rights. The African National Congress (ANC) fought against apartheid.

The road to freedom

ANC leader Nelson Mandela was imprisoned for 27 years for trying to end apartheid. When he was released in 1990, talks between the ANC and the South African government began. Apartheid ended, and Mandela became the first black president of South Africa in 1994.

Nelson Mandela at an election rally in Durban, South Africa, in 1994

In 1954, an American law was passed that ended segregation in schools.

Cold War

More than 200,000 flights were needed to support West Berlin.

After 1945, a struggle began between capitalist and communist countries. Under communism, the state owns all industries and property so that goods and housing can be shared out equally. Under capitalism, people can run their own businesses to make money. The capitalist USA and communist USSR were the war's biggest enemies.

Berlin Blockade and Airlift

In 1948–1949, communist East Germany stopped necessary supplies getting to capitalist West Berlin. The USA and its allies came to the city's aid. They used aircraft to bring goods into the area in an operation called the Berlin Airlift.

The USA supported capitalist South Korea during the Korean War (1950–1953), using tanks such as this one.

The two sides

Nations on each side made agreements, or treaties, to support one another in war. The capitalists formed a group called NATO. The Warsaw Pact united the USSR and other communist countries, such as Poland.

Badge of the Warsaw Pact, founded in 1955

Flag of NATO (North Atlantic Treaty Organization), founded in 1949

How did the Cold War get its name?

Nuclear weapons

Both sides built up their stocks of weapons, including nuclear missiles that could wipe out entire cities. No one launched a nuclear bomb in case the other side fired back. This was called Mutually Assured Destruction.

European uprisings

Under communism, people often weren't free to leave their country and faced problems such as food shortages. Tanks and troops from the USSR stopped people who protested against the government in Hungary in 1956 and in Czechoslovakia (now Slovakia and the Czech Republic) in 1968.

Protesters in Budapest, Hungary, in 1956

This gigantic nuclear missile made in the USSR is capable of flying a long distance to enemy territory.

The USA used helicopters to land troops in Vietnam.

Turn and learn
Communism
pp. 98–99

Vietnam War

Communist North Vietnam and capitalist South Vietnam fought a war against each other from 1955 to 1975. The USSR and China supported the North and the USA supported the South, which lost the war.

End of the Cold War

In 1989, people in communist Europe began to protest again. They pulled down the wall dividing East and West Berlin in Germany, took over the media, and threw communists out of governments.

East German people celebrate their freedom on top of the Berlin Wall in 1989.

Because the USA an USSR did not fight each other directly.

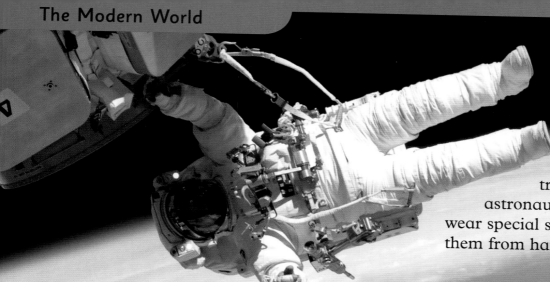

Astronauts
It takes months of training to become an astronaut. Once in space, they wear special spacesuits to protect them from harsh conditions.

Space exploration

People have always wondered what lies beyond planet Earth. However, it wasn't until the 1950s that space exploration began. Even today, with technology advancing all the time, we are really only at the beginning of discovering space.

The race to space
During the 1950s and 1960s, the USSR and the USA were in fierce competition to become the first nation to send a person into space.

| OCTOBER 1957 | NOVEMBER 1957 | APRIL 1961 | JULY 1969 |

The USSR put *Sputnik 1* into orbit to investigate Earth's atmosphere. It was the first ever artificial satellite to reach space.

Laika the dog was launched into space in 1957. She travelled on *Sputnik 2*, and was the first animal to fly around the Earth.

Yuri Gagarin was the first astronaut in outer space. He orbited the Earth during the USSR mission *Vostok 1*.

Americans Buzz Aldrin and Neil Armstrong became the first people on the Moon in the *Apollo 11* space mission.

How long did it take *Apollo 11* to get to the Moon and back?

Studying space

Scientists use satellites and probes to find out about space. Voyager 1 is a robotic spacecraft that was sent into space in 1977. It has now travelled so far that it has left the Solar System.

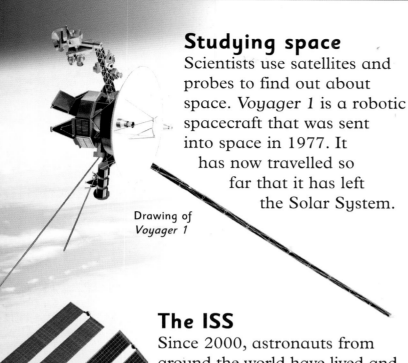

Drawing of
Voyager 1

Getting to space

Rockets launch astronauts, rovers, and satellites into space. They blast off by burning rocket fuel, which produces a burst of gas that pushes the rocket up.

Space shuttle *Atlantis*, first launched in 1985

The ISS

Since 2000, astronauts from around the world have lived and worked in the International Space Station (ISS) – a huge spacecraft that orbits, or travels around, Earth. It is the largest space station ever built.

The International
Space Station (ISS)

Solar panels provide
power to the ISS.

Missions on Mars

Special cars, called rovers, have been dropped onto Mars to explore its surface since 1976. The rover *Opportunity* has been there since 2004.

The Mars rover
Opportunity

The rover carries specialist
equipment, including a
robotic arm.

115

The mission took about eight days.

The United Nations flag

Changing world

The last few decades have brought huge changes across the world. Cheap air travel, new ways of communicating, and the end of communism allowed people to travel to, work in, and trade with more countries. Many countries also became democracies (where people vote for their leaders).

United Nations

During World War II, the United Nations organization was formed to encourage world peace. The 193 countries that belong to it try to end wars and to help people in places affected by conflict or other issues.

Parliament building in Gaborone, Botswana

Democracy in Africa

Many African countries were ruled by harsh, unfair governments. People fought for democracy, and some countries, such as Botswana, have remained democratic for more than 50 years. However, some parts of Africa still suffer from poverty and rule by unfair leaders.

China opens for business

Once cut off from the Western world due to communism, China now trades (buys and sells goods) with countries all over the world. European and American businesses have offices and factories in China.

Shanghai, a city in China, has lots of modern tower blocks. Foreign companies have offices here.

116

What do people mean by the term "global village"?

Globalization

Everything from air travel to the internet means that companies can trade easily across international borders. For example, cars made in Japan are sold all over the world. This is known as globalization.

Robots in a Japanese factory make cars that are sold worldwide.

Pizza is an Italian dish that spread to the USA in the 19th century, and it is now eaten worldwide.

The USSR collapses

Mikhail Gorbachev became leader of the USSR (Union of Soviet Socialist Republics) in 1985. He made communism in the USSR less strict, but the countries he ruled over wanted to be independent. The USSR broke apart in 1991.

Mikhail Gorbachev was the last leader of the USSR.

Cultural exchange

Improved communications and technology, globalization, and the spread of large businesses have meant that food, music, and brands from different cultures and countries are now recognized around the world.

The idea that technology, such as the internet, makes the world seem like a small place.

Technology

Our lives have been changed by modern technology. Computers and the internet have been invented, which link the world together. Technology has allowed scientists to create better medicines, wiping out diseases that were once incurable. It has also led to many new inventions.

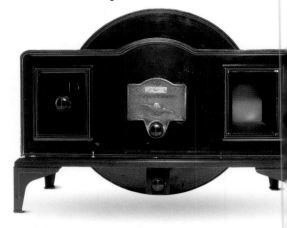

The first television was invented by John Logie Baird in the 1920s.

Home media
Television brought moving pictures into homes in the 1920s. The first televisions were large, expensive, and had tiny screens that had blurred pictures. By the 1950s, they were smaller, clearer, and cheaper.

Computer room from the 1960s

Small laptops with batteries that could be recharged became popular in the 1990s.

Getting connected
Satellites first orbited, or went around, the Earth in the 1950s. They were used to carry radio and television signals, or to gather scientific information, such as weather patterns. Today, they also carry internet and phone signals.

Computers
When computers were first invented after World War II, they were so big that one machine filled a whole room. They were used mainly in science laboratories and big businesses. It was not until the late 1970s that smaller computers, which could be used at home, were introduced.

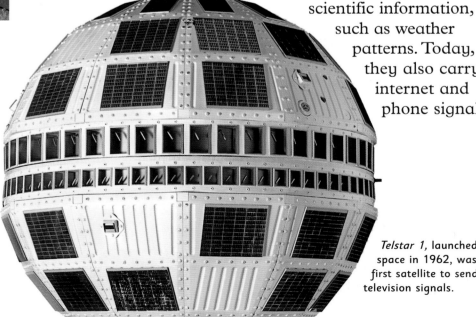

Telstar 1, launched in space in 1962, was the first satellite to send television signals.

What types of jobs can robots be used for?

Workers talking to a colleague in a different country, using the internet

Modern technology

Robots are machines that are powered by electric motors. They do tasks that are usually done by humans. Simple robots were first used in factories in the 1960s. Robots are now more advanced, and some have been sent to work in space.

The internet

First used in the 1960s, the internet is a network that links computers together. It now has millions of users around the world. The internet allows people to contact each other and to find information and entertainment.

The NAO robot was developed in 2006 by Aldebaran Robotics, a French robotics company. It can understand human speech, dance, and sense human faces.

Smartphones first came out in 2007

Mobile phones

Wireless, or mobile, phones were created in the 1980s to replace landline telephones, which are connected to a wall by a wire. Smartphones were introduced in the 2000s. They allow people to access the internet.

Some are used to help doctors with operations, and some help soldiers remove bombs.

Today's world

The world today faces many challenges, from wars and the changing climate to bad governments. However, advances in science and new political movements have led to improvements in the lives of millions of people.

Wind turbines convert (change) the wind's energy into electricity.

Renewable energy

The wind, waves, tides, and sunlight can all be used to generate (make) electricity. These are renewable sources of energy because they won't run out. Today, in 2019, around 20 per cent of electricity is made this way.

Car exhausts release carbon dioxide into the air.

Climate change

The general weather of a place makes up its climate. Greenhouse gases, such as carbon dioxide, are causing the Earth's climate to heat up. This melts ice sheets, making sea levels rise, and causes extreme weather, such as storms.

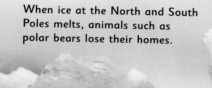

When ice at the North and South Poles melts, animals such as polar bears lose their homes.

What is our main source of energy?

Vaccines stop people from getting certain diseases.

Medical advances

New medicines are wiping out many diseases, and modern technology is making operations safer and easier. People in many places are living longer and leading healthier lives than in the past.

Global crisis

In 2008, banks in the USA began to fail. As a result, many people lost their jobs. The problems spread around the world, leading to riots, strikes (refusal to work), and even governments being replaced.

There were riots and strikes in the Greek capital city of Athens when the country suffered badly during the 2008 crisis.

Turn and learn

Independence
pp. 108–109
Technology
pp. 118–119

New nations

Some countries are still ruled by foreign powers or by leaders that have not been chosen by the people. However, people are winning the right to vote for their governments. New independent nations have also been formed recently.

People of South Sudan celebrate their country's independence in 2011.

121

Fossil fuels (coal, gas, or oil), which create greenhouse gases and will one day run out.

Timelines

Here are some people, inventions, and places that have changed history.

Kings and queens of England

These are some of the key rulers. The dates show when they were on the throne.

William I (1066–1087) Born in Normandy, France, William "the Conqueror" conquered England in 1066. He built the Tower of London and set up a system of government that lasted for hundreds of years.

Richard I (1189–1199) Known as "the Lionheart" for his bravery, he spent a lot of his rule abroad fighting a crusade, a Christian war against Muslims.

John (1199–1216) He signed a document known as Magna Carta ("Great Chapter"), which limited the king's power.

Henry VIII (1509–1547) Famous for his six wives, Henry made himself head of the Church of England.

Elizabeth I (1558–1603) Elizabeth ruled with great skill. She encouraged exploration and the arts, and her navy defended the country from a Spanish invasion.

James I (1603–1625) Already king of Scotland when he came to the English throne, James was the first to rule both Scotland and England.

Victoria (1837–1901)
Queen Victoria ruled for 64 years. She was queen when Britain was the world's richest and most powerful nation.

Queen Victoria

George VI (1936–1952)
George became king when his brother Edward VIII gave up the throne. He was a respected ruler during World War II.

Elizabeth II (1952–present day) The current queen has become the longest reigning monarch and is head of the Commonwealth (former colonies). Elizabeth II is a popular figure around the world.

Inventions

The wheel (c.3500 BCE)
The wheel was probably invented in Mesopotamia. The first wheels were potters' wheels; then people worked out how to use them to make chariots and carts.

Money (c.2000 BCE)
To begin with, people bought and sold by swapping things. The first forms of money were used in China and were small cowrie shells.

Early cart wheel

Paper (2nd century BCE) Paper was invented in China, but did not spread to Europe (where people wrote on parchment made from animal skins) for hundreds of years.

Car (1769) The first car, built in France by engineer Nicolas Cugnot, had a steam engine. Petrol-driven cars began to appear in the 1870s.

Vaccines (1796) British doctor Edward Jenner successfully tested the first vaccine against smallpox in 1796. Vaccination spread widely after this date.

Telephone (1876) Several inventors made telephones in the 19th century, but the one made by Alexander Graham Bell in 1876 was the one that people began to use. It took decades for telephones to become common because networks of wires had to be installed.

Light bulb (1879) Several inventors, including British Joseph Swan and American Thomas Edison, invented working light bulbs in the 1870s.

Aeroplane (1903) American brothers Wilbur and Orville Wright made the first successful flights in a small engine-powered aeroplane in 1903. Their aircraft, the *Flyer*, had canvas wings, a lightweight frame, and a tiny engine.

Space rocket (1944) The first rocket that got into space was the German V2, a missile used in warfare. By the 1950s, rockets were being used to carry satellites into space for peaceful purposes.

World Wide Web (1989)
The World Wide Web is a collection of pages of information on the internet. It was invented by Tim Berners-Lee and other scientists, and made the internet easy for everyone to use.

Early light bulb

Historical sites

Stonehenge, England (c.3000–1520 BCE)
The most famous ancient stone circle was built as a religious site. Its biggest stones are 9 metres (30 feet) tall and were constructed using only simple tools.

Pyramids of Giza, Egypt (c.2600–2500 BCE)
The pyramids formed the burial places of the ancient Egyptian pharaohs. The biggest, the Great Pyramid, is 147 metres (482 feet) high, and was the tomb of Pharaoh Khufu.

The Pyramids of Giza

Great Wall of China (c.215–212 BCE)
Begun in the 3rd century BCE, the Great Wall of China was continually improved. By the end of the Ming Dynasty (1644), the wall was as it is today, stretching 8,850 km (5,499 miles) across northern China.

Parthenon, Athens (447 BCE)
The most famous temple in ancient Greece, the Parthenon is in Athens. It is the temple of Athena, goddess of war and wisdom and protector of the city.

Walls of Constantinople, Istanbul, Turkey (5th century BCE)
These walls, up to 12 metres (39 feet) tall, helped Constantinople survive many attacks before the Ottoman Turkish army finally broke through and conquered the city in 1453.

Petra, Jordan (4th century BCE to 1st century CE)
This city was the capital of the Nabatean people. They cut many of their buildings out of tall sandstone cliffs, hollowing rooms out of the solid rock.

Colosseum, Rome (72–80 CE)
This huge Roman amphitheatre is about 189 metres (620 feet) across and could hold up to 80,000 people. Contests between gladiators were held in its arena and were a popular form of entertainment in ancient Rome.

Pompeii (79 CE)
Pompeii is an ancient Roman town that was preserved when covered in ash from a volcano in 79 CE.

Hadrian's Wall (122 CE)
The Romans built Hadrian's Wall across the north of Britain to stop attacks from tribes who lived further north. It was a huge task to build it, because it is in rocky and hilly country, away from towns.

Key turning points

Cities (c.4500 BCE)
When the first big cities were built, human life began to change. It was less focused on the countryside, and more people were learning specialized crafts or working as traders.

Writing (c.3400–3000 BCE)
The first writing systems were invented in ancient Egypt and Mesopotamia. They allowed people to record trade deals, to write down poetry and fiction, and to exchange their ideas with other people.

Bronzeworking (c.3500 BCE)
When people started using bronze, they created new weapons, tools, and styles of jewellery. This first happened in western Asia.

Printed words (c.200 CE)
The Chinese printed the first books, using carved wooden blocks. In the 15th century, Johannes Gutenberg in Germany invented a printing press using metal type (letters).

Renaissance (14th century onwards)
The Renaissance was a movement in European culture that led to more realistic art, but also encouraged improvements in education and science.

Gregorian telescope

Optics (c.1600)
In around 1600, people discovered how to make telescopes and microscopes using glass lenses, which made objects look bigger. This opened up huge new areas of discovery in science and astronomy.

Enlightenment (late-17th to early-18th century)
A new movement in thinking, the Enlightenment, began in western Europe. Enlightenment writers and scientists insisted that people use reason and evidence in their research, rather than just drawing information from religious teachings.

Evolution (1859)
British scientist Charles Darwin developed the theory of evolution. This explains how living things evolve (change over time) to help them survive in their environment.

Germ theory (1860s)
French scientist Louis Pasteur discovered the role of germs in carrying disease. This led to advances in medicine and the treatment of previously incurable illnesses.

Charles Darwin

True or false?

Can you work out which of these
facts are real and which ones are
completely made up?

2 The Celtic queen Boudicca fought the Romans in 60 CE.

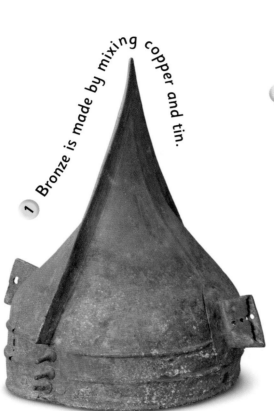

1 Bronze is made by mixing copper and tin.

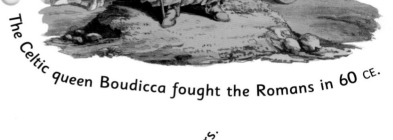

4 The International Space Station (ISS) orbits Mars.

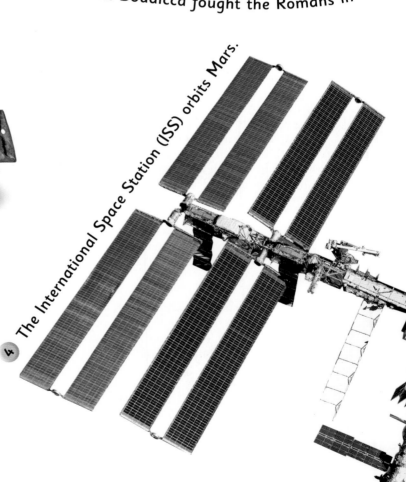

3 Caliphs were leaders who ruled the Islamic empire.

124

5 Sargon was a pharaoh from ancient Egypt.

6 Zeus was the ancient Roman god of fire.

7 Women in the USA won the right to vote by 1920.

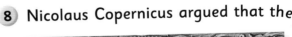

8 Nicolaus Copernicus argued that the planets moved around the Sun.

Answers: 1: True 2: True 3: True 4: False – it orbits the Earth. 5: False – he was a ruler from Akkad.

Quiz

Test your knowledge of history with these tricky quiz questions.

4 Which of the following is a form of renewable energy?

A: Exhaust fumes   **B: Sunlight**

C: Electricity   **D: Fire**

5 Which dynasty did ancient China's first emperor belong to?

A: Song   **B: Tang**

C: Qin   **D: Shang**

1 Which animal did people hunt for meat and warm skins during the Ice Age?

A: Woolly mammoth **B: Elephant**

C: Sheep   **D: Giant ground sloth**

2 Which sea battle off the coast of Greece was a crushing defeat for the Turks?

A: Battle of Panipat   **B: Battle of Saratoga**

C: Battle of Lepanto   **D: Battle of Gettysburg**

6 Which military commander during the French Revolution later became the emperor of France?

A: Louis XVI   **B: Marie Antoinette**

C: Henry VIII   **D: Napoleon Bonaparte**

3 What event started the American Revolution?

A: Gold rush   **B: Storming the Bastille**

C: Boston Tea Party   **D: Battle of the Somme**

7 What is the Korean script called?

A: Hieroglyphs   **B: Hangul**

C: Calligraphy   **D: Cuneiform**

8 Which flower is worn in memory of all soldiers who have died during wars?

A: Rose

B: Poppy

C: Petunia

D: Lily

9 What did the East India Company trade in Indonesia?

A: Chocolate

B: Furs

C: Fish

D: Spices

10 What were the symbols of industry and agriculture during the Russian Revolution?

A: Communist posters

B: Stars and stripes

C: Hammer and sickle

D: Stars and bars

11 Who is the Aztec god of war?

A: Quetzalcoatl

B: Huitzilopochtli

C: Tlaloc

D: Viracocha

12 Which Reformation leader translated the Bible into German?

A: John Calvin

B: John Knox

C: Henry VIII

D: Martin Luther

13 What disease was the rat responsible for spreading in the 14th century?

A: Smallpox

B: Diphtheria

C: Measles

D: Black Death

14 What was the religion of the ancient Persians?

A: Zoroastrianism

B: Shamanism

C: Confucianism

D: Buddhism

15 Which Portuguese explorer was the first to reach the Indian coast?

A: Vasco da Gama

B: Christopher Columbus

C: James Cook

D: Ferdinand Magellan

16 Who made the famous "I have a dream" speech about a future USA with equal rights for all?

A: Rosa Parks

B: Martin Luther King Jr

C: Malcolm X

D: Nelson Mandela

Answers: 1: A 2: C 3: C 4: B 5: C 6: C 7: D 8: B 9: D 10: C 11: B 12: D 13: D 14: A 15: A 16: B

Who or what am I?

Can you work out who or what is being talked about from each clue?

Viking warrior

2: I travelled by sea to find new lands to raid.

Tutankhamun

Augustus

Gladiator

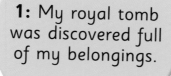

1: My royal tomb was discovered full of my belongings.

Rameses II

Telegraph

Cyrus the Great

German Enigma machine

Mongol horseman

Taro plant

Rice plant

3: I am an important crop planted by the Polynesians.

Knight

Papyrus

Al-Zahrawi's book On Surgery and Instruments

Diamond Sutra

Smartphone

Telstar 1 satellite

5: I am the world's oldest surviving printed book.

4: I was used to send instant messages during the US Civil War.

Mao Zedong's Little Red Book

Gutenberg Bible

1: This traditional Inuit statue is used in Canada as a symbol of hope and friendship.

2: A statue of this president, who helped free slaves, stands in Washington, D.C., USA.

3: The Anglo-Saxons built this church in Northamptonshire, UK.

4: The Maya built this pyramid in Chichén Itzá, Mexico.

5: Ancient Romans built this aqueduct to bring fresh water to Nîmes, France.

6: The Incas of Peru built this citadel high in the Andes Mountains.

Where in the world?

Match the description of the landmark or person to the pictures and discover where in the world they can be found.

Pont du Gard

James Cook

The Kaaba

Machu Picchu

Abraham Lincoln

Brixworth Church

7: Hagia Sophia 8: Emperor Meiji 9: The Kaaba 10: Taj Mahal 11: James Cook 12: Djinguereber Mosque

7: Completed in 537 CE in Constantinople (modern-day Istanbul), this Byzantine church was once the largest in the world.

8: Situated in Mecca, Saudi Arabia, this is the most holy Islamic site.

9: This ruler became the emperor of Japan at the young age of 15.

10: This tomb in India is one of the most impressive examples of Mughal architecture.

12: This place in Timbuktu used to be a site for scholars and students.

11: This British explorer sailed to Australia on his search for new lands in the southern Pacific Ocean.

Djinguereber Mosque

Emperor Meiji

Hagia Sophia

El Castillo

The Inukshuk

Taj Mahal

Answers: 1: The Inukshuk 2: Abraham Lincoln 3: Brixworth Church 4: El Castillo 5: Pont du Gard 6: Machu Picchu

Glossary

afterlife second life that some people believe will happen after they die

archaeology finding out about the past by looking at remains, often those dug up out of the ground

aristocracy highest class of people in some societies

astronomer person who studies the sky and the stars

campaign take actions towards a particular goal

capitalism way of life where businesses are owned by individuals so that they can make money for themselves

ceremonies special, often religious, set of acts

city-state city that runs itself and is not a part of another country or state

civilization society or group of people who share the same way of life

class (social) label given to a person in society due to their wealth and job. People with more money and higher-paid jobs are considered higher class than those with less money

colonies areas ruled by other countries

colonize send people to a place and gain control over it

communism way of life where property and industries belong to the government or state. The wealth of the state is divided equally among its people

conquer take control of a place by force, usually through battle

crusade war fought by medieval Christians against people of other religions

dwelling place where a person lives

dynasty ruling family whose rule is passed down to the following generations

emperor ruler of an empire

empire group of lands or nations ruled by one leader or government

expedition long trip a person would go on, often to explore

exploration trying to discover or find out about something or somewhere

feudal system medieval system in which lords allowed people of lower rank to hold land, in return for services

furnace big oven used for heating and melting materials

indigenous people group of people who were living somewhere before settlers took over the land

industry organization that produces (makes) something

invade enter a country or area in large numbers, using force to seize control of it

merchant person who sells goods or trades with other people to make money

monarch king or queen

monk man who dedicates his life to his religion. Monks usually live in a monastery

movement group of people working together to make change

nation community of people who share the same history

navigation finding a route at sea or on land, usually using maps

orbit path that something makes around another object in space

ornament object used for decoration

parchment used for writing on before paper was invented. It was made from the skin of an animal.

plateau big area of flat land

poverty not having enough money to take care of basic needs, such as food

probe small spacecraft, without people inside, sent to explore space

prophet religious teacher, thought to be a messenger of God by their followers

protest showing that you do not agree or approve of something

revolution sudden overthrowing of a system of rule or way of life

ritual religious activity where people perform a set of actions

sacred linked to one God or gods

sacrifice killing an animal or person for a religious ceremony

satellite object that orbits a larger object in space

scholar person who is considered an expert in a subject

settlers group of people who move to live in another place or country

surrender to give up

tax money paid by people to their government, to fund services, such as hospitals

territory area of land that belongs to a ruler or state

trade buy and sell. Can also mean swapping goods

treaty agreement signed by the leaders of two or more nations

vaccine medicine given to people to prevent a disease, usually by an injection

warfare act of fighting a war or being involved in conflict

Stone statues called *Moai* found on Easter Island

Index

Picture credits

The publisher would like to thank the following for their kind permission to reproduce their images:

(Key: a-above; c-centre; b-below; l-left; r-right; t-top)

123RF.com: Chelovek 112bc, jezper 120tr, liligraphie 4tl, Sborisov 77b, Scott Fensome / zollster 97crb, 127tl; akg-images: 112tl, 113cr; Alamy Stock Photo: Photo 12 89tc, 109tc, Art Collection 2 63cr, 83tc, 360b 24-25, 125cra, FLHC 8 56clb, 129c, Adwo 39tl, Ancient Art and Architecture 23cl, Granger Historical Picture Archive 1, 20bl, 42cr, 67br, 74clb, 87bl, 98-99, 100-101b, 102-103, 103crb, Roger Arnold 99cr, Art Directors & TRIP 41cra, Derek Bayes / Lebrecht Music & Arts 38crb, Peter Barritt 43bl, 130br (Brixworth Saxon Church), Sabena Jane Blackbird 37cla, Tibor Bognar 58cr, Agencja Fotograficzna Caro 113bl, Chronicle 33bc, 59bl, 85bl, 92b, 124cra, 131bl (Emperor Meiji), Thomas Cockrem 109b, ColsTravel 69tc, IanDagnall Computing 79cla, Joshua Davenport 60-61, dbimages 70-71b, 127cr, Design Pics Inc 109cl, 131br (Stone Inuksuk), Benedicte Desrus 121br, Niels Poulsen DK 45crb, Wilf Doyle 103tl, Adam Eastland 77tc, Reiner Elsen 18-19bl, Everett Collection Inc 102bl, EyeSee Microstock 31cr, AF Fotografie 75crb, Age Fotostock 57cr, 75tl, Corentin LE GALL 54-55, Les Gibbon 9crb, Tuul & Bruno Morandi / mauritius images GmbH 55tr, The Granger Collection 87c, 91br, Peter J. Hatcher 43tr, Heritage Image Partnership Ltd 33cr, 52tr, 124bl, Hirarchivum Press 19crb, History and Art Collection 85cr, The History Collection 85tr, 101tl, imageBROKER 9bl, Abbus Archive Images 57cla, Archive Images 75clb, INTERFOTO 104bl, 111tr, ITAR-TASS News Agency 117c, Keystone Pictures USA 113tc, Lanmas 11br, Lebrecht Music & Arts 92cra, cai liang 20crb, Lucy Brown (loca4motion) 55b, Stefano Politi Markovina 22cra (Ionic column), Jeff Morgan 01 4b, William Mullins 69cl, Eric Nathan 105cra, The Natural History Museum 84c, Niday Picture Library 51tr, 79crb, North Wind Picture Archives 22b, 78clb, 78clb (John Calvin), 78bl, 95crb, Yooran Park 60clb, Dinodia Photos 82c, 108bl, Pictorial Press Ltd 70bl, 93tl, 103cla, 103bc, The Picture Art Collection 20cla, 26tr, 53tl, 90bl, 126cr, 128bc (Cyrus II), PjrTravel 99br, Pamela Reynolds 91cra, Hans-Joachim Schneider 61tl, Science History Images 33cla, 49bc, 51clb, 51br, 77tl, 95tl, 96tl, 107clb, 118cl, 125br, Christopher Scott 63b, Jana Shea 101br, SPUTNIK 114cb, Steve Allen Travel Photography 68-69, 130bc (Inca citadel), Travelpass Photography 15crb, Universal Images Group North America LLC 107cra, V&A Images 72br, 93crb, Lucas Vallecillos 81cra, VintageCorner 106cl, Edward Westmacott 42l, Jan Wlodarczyk 16-17bc, 128clb, World History Archive 15tl, 25cr, 45bl, 52br, 73tc, 76cl, 79bl, 80br, 81cr, 100cra, 129cra, Ming WU 21b, www. BibleLandPictures.com 11bl, 125cla, Philipp Zechner 59ca; © The Board of Trustees of the Armouries: Tim Ridley 129cla; Bridgeman Images: A map of America and Canada, from 'A New General Atlas, containing a Geographical and and Historical Account of all the Empires, Kingdoms and other Dominions of the World...', 1721 (colour litho), Senex, John (1678-1740) / British Library, London, UK / © British Library Board. All Rights Reserved 72-73tc, Pictures from History 56tr, Iraq: Arabic manuscript illumination from the 13th century CE showing philosophers belonging to the Ikhwan al-Safa or 'Brethren of Purity' / Pictures from History 53tr; The Trustees of the British Museum: 27cra, 64b; Depositphotos Inc: Frizio 15cb, Borna_mir 26b; Dorling Kindersley: Andy Crawford / Trustees of the National Museums Of Scotland 52clb, © The Board of Trustees of the Armouries 55tl, © The Board of Trustees of the Armouries 55tc, © The Board of Trustees of the Armouries 55ca, The Trustees of the British Museum 55c, The Trustees of the British Museum 64b, The Trustees of the British Museum 69tl, Wilberforce House, Hull City Museums 74-75c, By permission of The British Library and By permission of The British Library 78tr, © The Board of Trustees of the Armouries 80cl, © The Board of Trustees of the Armouries 80fcl, Amit Pashricha / National Museum, New Delhi 82clb, © The Board of Trustees of the Armouries 87t, The Trustees of the British

Museum 89cr, State Central Museum of Contemporary History of Russia 98bl, Tim Ridley / © The Board of Trustees of the Armouries 129cla, 129br, 130bl, American Museum of Natural History 65tc, Board of Trustees of the Royal Armouries 46bl, Bolton Library and Museum Services / Norman Taylor 15cra (Ring), Bolton Metro Museum / Peter Anderson 16l, Booth Museum of Natural History, Brighton / Tim Parmenter 13tc, Cairo Museum 17br, 128cla, Canterbury City Council, Museums and Galleries / Gary Ombler 9cra, Canterbury City Council, Museums and Galleries / Richard Leeney 73clb, The Combined Military Services Museum (CMSM) 32tr, CONACULTA-INAH-MEX 36cl, 67cr, Courtesy of Royal Museum of the Armed Forces and of Military History, Brussels, Belgium 112clb, Andy Crawford 35cb, 51c, Durham University Oriental Museum 56br, 61tr, 61cra, 61cb, 61crb, 61bc, 61fcrb, 81bc, 126br, Durham University Oriental Museum / Dave King 59tr, Durham University Oriental Museum / Gary Ombler 10tr, 82br, 83cla, Gettysburg National Military Park, PA 94-95b, Glasgow Museum 118tr, Hastings Borough Council 65tl, Hellenic Maritime Museum 23b, Imperial War Museum, London 98cl, 106cra, 128bc (Enigma), Peter Keim 87crb, 94cra, Maidstone Museum and Bentliff Art Gallery 43c, Maidstone Museum and Bentliff Art Gallery / Richard Leeney 58br, 58l, Museum of London 32cra, Museum of London / Dave King 19ca, NASA 114cra, National Music Museum 77tr, Natural History Museum, London 39cra, 63ca, Natural History Museum, London / Colin Keates 52bc, Newcastle Great Northern Museum 31tl, Newcastle Great Northern Museum, Hancock 25ca, 43br, Oxford Museum of Natural History / Gary Ombler 6cla, Oxford University Museum of Natural History / Gary Ombler 19cra, John Pearce 97ca, Pitt Rivers Museum, University of Oxford 39crb, 85tl, 93clb, Powell Cotton Museum, Quex Park 62c, RAF Cosford 105cl, Royal Airforce Museum, London 97c, Scale Model World, Thomas Poelkemauu 105c, Science Museum, London 90tr, The Science Museum, London 118br, 129cb, The Science Museum, London / Dave King 122tr, 122br, Southern Skirmish Association 95clb, The Tank Museum, Bovington 106br, Thackeray Medical Museum 77ca, 77ca (Drug jar), The University of Aberdeen 24cl, 75tr, The University of Aberdeen / Gary Ombler 4c, 15cra, 73c, University Museum of Archaeology and Anthropology, Cambridge 33clb, University Museum of Archaeology and Anthropology, Cambridge / Dave King 12cra, 19cra (Pin & Mould), 19cl, University of Pennsylvania Museum of Archaeology and Anthropology 37br, 41tc, 49c, 49c (Coin 2), 49c (Coin 3), 62br, 69cra, 93cl, 93cr, University of Pennsylvania Museum of Archaeology and Anthropology / Angela Coppola 19tc, University of Pennsylvania Museum of Archaeology and Anthropology / Gary Ombler 19c, 73bl, 124cl, Vikings of Middle England 44br, Whipple Museum of History of Science, Cambridge 123cr; Dreamstime.com: 118c, Ahmad Faizal Yahya / Afby71 41tl, 130bc (Kaaba), Airphoto 14clb, Stig Alenäs 48tr, Andreykuzmin 70-71 (Background), Anyaivanova 24b, Anthony Baggett / Tonybaggett 5cl, Robert Zehetmayer / Bertl123 29b, Bryan Busovicki /Tank_bmb 76br, Artur Bogacki 11tl, Borna Mirahmadian / Borna 27clb, Burij 23tl, Chinaview 57tr, Andrew Churchill 116tl, Ifeelstock / iPhone is a trademark of Apple Inc., registered in the U.S. and other countries 119clb, 129clb, Danbreckwoldt / Dan Breckwoldt 123cla, Diegophoto / Diego Elorza 17cra, Dinosmichail 49cra, Regien Paassen / Dzain 28-29c, Edwardgerges 15clb, Elgreko74 25tl, Ewamewa2 13crb, Frenta 31br, Jose Gil 86bl, Scott Griessel 22cr, Tetiana Guzhva 5bc, Havana1234 97br, Nataliya Hora 29cla, Hugoht 71cra, Miroslav Jacimovic 28b, 128ca, Jasonjung 9cb, Bohuslav Jelen 99ca, Jeremyreds 36-37b, 131bc (Chichen Itza), Joools 71tc, Panagiotis Karapanagiotis 22cra, Georgios Kollidas 122bc, Larysole 95cb, 128crb, Ldprod 119tl, Yiu Tung Lee 41bc, Libux77 70-71 (Map), Liorpt 40bc, Netfalls 31tr, Nevinates 35cb (Cinnamon), Boonlong Noragitt 30t, Radiokafka 27crb, Tauha2001 23tl (Olives), Thom800 15clb (Fig), Lev Tsimbler 25bc, Woravit Vijitpanya 15cl, 23ftl, Alvaro German Vilela 53bl, Wisconsinart 21tl, Robert Zehetmayer 48-49, 131bc (Hagia Sophia), Zhiwei Zhou 57b, Zhudifeng 116-117b, Znm 14cla, 129cla (Papyrus), Zwawol 47br; Getty Images: AFP Contributor 108cra, Jimmy Sime / Central Press / Hulton Archive 100bl, Per-Anders Pettersson / Hulton Archive 111br, Michael Ochs Archives 110clb

(Martin Luther King, Jr), Bettmann 107br, Bloomberg 117tl, Kiyoshi Ota / Bloomberg 119r, Central Press / Hulton Archive 112-113c, Christophel Fine Art / UIG 47tl, CM Dixon / Print Collector 66tr, Print Collector 89cr, Corbis 105tl, Don Cravens / The LIFE Images Collection 111cla, DEA / A. DAGLI ORTI / De Agostini 13tl, 13cla, DEA / G. DAGLI ORTI / De Agostini 66-67, DEA PICTURE LIBRARY / De Agostini 67tc, DEA PICTURE LIBRARY / De Agostini Picture Library 73cb, DeAgostini 50b, Paul Souders / Corbis Documentary 120-121bl, Fine Art Images / Heritage Images 96br, fotog 94bl, 130br (Lincoln Memorial), Fox Photos / Hulton Archive 32c, 32b, Geoffrey Malins / IWM 97t, Ken Florey Suffrage Collection / Gado 101cl, 125cl, Leemage 89l, Leemage / Corbis 2-3b, 34-35b, De Agostini / W. Buss / De Agostini Picture Library 12-13bl, DEA PICTURE LIBRARY 55cr, 88b, Sergio Momo 54clb, 129tl, Ralph Morse / The LIFE Picture Collection 8-9tc, Milos Bicanski / Getty Images News 121cra, Bob Parent / Archive Photos 110bl, Photo 12 / Universal Images Group 110clb (Rosa Parks), Eggit / Fox Photos 105br, Robert W. Kelley / The LIFE Picture Collection 110-111b, 127br, Robert Harding / robertharding 13c, Robin Smith 35t, Smith Collection / Gado 95tr, Stocktrek Images 115tl, John van Hasselt / Sygma 61c, Universal History Archive / UIG 34cl, UniversalImagesGroup 88cla, Werner Forman / Universal Images Group 49tl; iStockphoto.com: andyKRAKOVSKI 69br, Photo_Concepts 121tl, kickstand 110tr, Lovattpics 116cl, Iwanami Photos 63tl, 131bl (Djinguereber Mosque); Library of Congress, Washington, D.C.: LC-DIG-ppmsca-39879 / D.F. Barry, June 1885 65br, LC-USZC4-523 / N. Currier (Firm) 86cr, LC-DIG-pga-08593 126bl, LC-DIG-ggbain-01084 / Bain News Service 101ca, LC-DIG-ggbain-30124 / Bain News Service 101ca (Susan B. Anthony), LC-USZC2-4067 101cl, LC-USZC4-2912 87ca; NASA: 114cb (Yuri Gagarin), JPL / Cornell University 115b, JSC 114, KSC 115ca, MSFC 115cl, 124-125bc; National Museum Of China: 20br; National Museum, New Delhi: Amit Pashricha 82clb; State Central Museum of Contemporary History of Russia: 98bl; SuperStock: Universal Images 27tl; The Metropolitan Museum of Art: Gift of Margaret Wishard, in memory of her mother, Mrs. Luther D. Wishard, 1974 59crb, Purchase, Caroline Howard Hyman Gift, in memory of Margaret English Frazer, 2000 19cla, Rogers Fund and Edward S. Harkness Gift, 1920 14-15bl, Rogers Fund, 1907 25cl, Rogers Fund, 1928 17tl; Trustees of the National Museums Of Scotland: Andy Crawford 52clb; Wellcome Images http://creativecommons.org/licenses/by/4.0/: 51tc

Cover images: Front: Alamy Stock Photo: Adam Eastland tl; Dorling Kindersley: Cairo Museum r, Paul Ford tr, Bob Gathany c; Getty Images: SSPL clb, Universal History Archive / UIG tc; The Metropolitan Museum of Art: Rogers Fund, 1907 tc/ (Bowl); Back: Dorling Kindersley: Durham University Oriental Museum cl, University Museum of Archaeology and Anthropology, Cambridge tc/ (Metalwork), University of Pennsylvania Museum of Archaeology and Anthropology tc/ (Collar); Getty Images: Ashmolean Museum / Heritage Images tc; The Metropolitan Museum of Art: Gift of Margaret Wishard, in memory of her mother, Mrs. Luther D. Wishard, 1974 crb; Spine: Dreamstime.com: Chikapylka ca; Getty Images: Schenectady Museum; Hall of Electrical History Foundation / Corbis t

All other images © Dorling Kindersley
For further information see: www.dkimages.com

Acknowledgements

Dorling Kindersley would like to thank: Caroline Hunt for proofreading; and Hilary Bird for indexing.